CAMBRIDGE LIBRARY COLLECTION

Books of enduring scholarly value

English Men of Letters

In the 1870s, Macmillan publishers began to issue a series of books called
'English Men of Letters' – biographies of English writers by other English
writers. The general editor of the series was the journalist, critic, politician,
and supporter (and later biographer) of Gladstone, John Morley (1838–
1923). The aim was to provide a short introduction to each subject and his
works, but also that the life should illuminate the works, and vice versa. The
subjects range chronologically from Chaucer to Thackeray and Dickens, and
an important feature of the series is that many of the authors (Henry James
on Hawthorne, Ward on Dickens) were discussing writers of the previous
generation, and some (Trollope on Thackeray) had even known their subjects
personally. The series exemplifies the British approach to literary biography
and criticism at the end of the nineteenth century, and also reveals which
authors were at that time regarded as canonical.

Bacon

This introduction to the life and works of Francis Bacon (1561–1626) was
published in the first series of English Men of Letters in 1884. The author,
R. W. Church (1815–90), who also wrote on Spenser for this series, begins
forcefully: 'The life of Francis Bacon is one which it is a pain to write or to
read. It is the life of a man endowed with as rare a combination of noble
gifts as ever was bestowed on a human intellect … And yet it was not only
an unhappy life; it was a poor life.' Church, while paying the highest tribute
to Bacon's intellectual achievements in so many different fields, argues that
'there was in Bacon's 'self' a deep and fatal flaw. He was a pleaser of men.' He
believed that this work should correct the adulatory stance adopted by earlier
biographers, and reveal the whole, imperfect man.

Cambridge University Press has long been a pioneer in the reissuing of out-of-print titles from its own backlist, producing digital reprints of books that are still sought after by scholars and students but could not be reprinted economically using traditional technology. The Cambridge Library Collection extends this activity to a wider range of books which are still of importance to researchers and professionals, either for the source material they contain, or as landmarks in the history of their academic discipline.

Drawing from the world-renowned collections in the Cambridge University Library, and guided by the advice of experts in each subject area, Cambridge University Press is using state-of-the-art scanning machines in its own Printing House to capture the content of each book selected for inclusion. The files are processed to give a consistently clear, crisp image, and the books finished to the high quality standard for which the Press is recognised around the world. The latest print-on-demand technology ensures that the books will remain available indefinitely, and that orders for single or multiple copies can quickly be supplied.

The Cambridge Library Collection will bring back to life books of enduring scholarly value (including out-of-copyright works originally issued by other publishers) across a wide range of disciplines in the humanities and social sciences and in science and technology.

Bacon

CAMBRIDGE UNIVERSITY PRESS

Cambridge, New York, Melbourne, Madrid, Cape Town,
Singapore, São Paolo, Delhi, Tokyo, Mexico City

Published in the United States of America by Cambridge University Press, New York

www.cambridge.org
Information on this title: www.cambridge.org/9781108034432

© in this compilation Cambridge University Press 2011

This edition first published 1884
This digitally printed version 2011

ISBN 978-1-108-03443-2 Paperback

English Men of Letters

EDITED BY JOHN MORLEY

BACON

BACON

BY

R. W. CHURCH,

DEAN OF ST. PAUL'S,
HONORARY FELLOW OF ORIEL COLLEGE

London:

MACMILLAN AND CO.

1884

PREFACE.

IN preparing this sketch it is needless to say how deeply I am indebted to Mr. Spedding and Mr. Ellis, the last editors of Bacon's writings, the very able and painstaking commentators, the one on Bacon's life, the other on his philosophy. It is impossible to overstate the affectionate care and high intelligence and honesty with which Mr. Spedding has brought together and arranged the materials for an estimate of Bacon's character. In the result, in spite of the force and ingenuity of much of his pleading, I find myself most reluctantly obliged to differ from him; it seems to me to be a case where the French saying, cited by Bacon, in one of his commonplace books, holds good—"*Par trop se débattre, la vérité se perd.*" [1] But this does not diminish the debt of gratitude which all who are interested about Bacon must owe to Mr. Spedding. I wish also to acknowledge the assistance which I have received from Mr. Gardiner's *History of England* and Mr. Fowler's edition of the *Novum Organum*: and not least from M. de Rémusat's work on Bacon, which seems to me the most complete and the most just estimate

---

[1] *Promus:* edited by Mrs. H. Pott, p. 475.

both of Bacon's character and work, which has yet appeared; though even in this clear and dispassionate survey we are reminded by some misconceptions, strange in M. de Rémusat, how what one nation takes for granted is incomprehensible to its neighbour, and what a gap there is still, even in matters of philosophy and literature, between the whole Continent and ourselves :—

"Penitus toto divisos orbe Britannos."

CONTENTS.

BACON.

CHAPTER I.

EARLY LIFE.

THE life of Francis Bacon is one which it is a pain to write or to read. It is the life of a man endowed with as rare a combination of noble gifts as ever was bestowed on a human intellect; the life of one with whom the whole purpose of living and of every day's work was to do great things to enlighten and elevate his race, to enrich it with new powers, to lay up in store for all ages to come a source of blessings which should never fail or dry up; it was the life of a man who had high thoughts of the ends and methods of law and government, and with whom the general and public good was regarded as the standard by which the use of public power was to be measured; the life of a man who had struggled hard and successfully for the material prosperity and opulence which makes work easy and gives a man room and force for carrying out his purposes. All his life long his first and never-sleeping passion was the romantic and splendid ambition after knowledge, for the conquest of nature and for the service of man; gathering up in himself the spirit and longings and efforts of

Œ   B

all discoverers and inventors of the arts, as they are symbolised in the mythical Prometheus. He rose to the highest place and honour; and yet that place and honour were but the fringe and adornment of all that made him great. It is difficult to imagine a grander and more magnificent career; and his name ranks among the few chosen examples of human achievement. And yet it was not only an unhappy life; it was a poor life. We expect that such an overwhelming weight of glory should be borne up by a character corresponding to it in strength and nobleness. But that is not what we find. No one ever had a greater idea of what he was made for, or was fired with a greater desire to devote himself to it. He was all this. And yet being all this, seeing deep into man's worth, his capacities, his greatness, his weakness, his sins, he was not true to what he knew. He cringed to such a man as Buckingham. He sold himself to the corrupt and ignominious Government of James I. He was willing to be employed to hunt to death a friend like Essex, guilty, deeply guilty to the State, but to Bacon the most loving and generous of benefactors. With his eyes open he gave himself up without resistance to a system unworthy of him; he would not see what was evil in it, and chose to call its evil good; and he was its first and most signal victim.

Bacon has been judged with merciless severity. But he has also been defended by an advocate whose name alone is almost a guarantee for the justness of the cause which he takes up, and the innocency of the client for whom he argues. Mr. Spedding devoted nearly a lifetime and all the resources of a fine intellect and an earnest conviction to make us revere as well as admire

Bacon. But it is vain. It is vain to fight against the facts of his life : his words, his letters. " Men are made up," says a keen observer, " of professions, gifts and talents ; and also of *themselves.*"[1] With all his greatness, his splendid genius, his magnificent ideas, his enthusiasm for truth, his passion to be the benefactor of his kind, with all the charm that made him loved by good and worthy friends, amiable, courteous, patient, delightful as a companion, ready to take any trouble,— there was in Bacon's " self " a deep and fatal flaw. He was a pleaser of men. There was in him that subtle fault, noted and named both by philosophy and religion, in the ἄρεσκος of Aristotle, the ἀνθρωπάρεσκος of St. Paul, which is more common than it is pleasant to think, even in good people, but which if it becomes dominant in a character is ruinous to truth and power. He was one of the men, there are many of them, who are unable to release their imagination from the impression of present and immediate power, face to face with themselves. It seems as if he carried into conduct the leading rule of his philosophy of nature, *parendo vincitur.* In both worlds, moral and physical, he felt himself encompassed by vast forces, irresistible by direct opposition. Men whom he wanted to bring round to his purposes were as strange, as refractory, as obstinate, as impenetrable as the phenomena of the natural world. It was no use attacking in front and by a direct trial of strength people like Elizabeth or Cecil or James : he might as well think of forcing some natural power in defiance of natural law. The first word of his teaching about nature is that she must be won by observation of

[1] Dr. Mozley.

her tendencies and demands ; the same radical disposition of temper reveals itself in his dealings with men ; they, too, must be won by yielding to them, by adapting himself to their moods and ends ; by spying into the drift of their humour, by subtly and pliantly falling in with it, by circuitous and indirect processes, the fruit of vigilance and patient thought. He thought to direct, while submitting apparently to be directed. But he mistook his strength. Nature and man are different powers and under different laws. He chose to please man, and not to follow what his soul must have told him was the better way. He wanted, in his dealings with men, that sincerity on which he insisted so strongly in his dealings with nature and knowledge. And the ruin of a great life was the consequence.

Francis Bacon was born in London on the 22d of January 15$\frac{60}{61}$, three years before Galileo. He was born at York House, in the Strand; the house which, though it belonged to the Archbishops of York, had been lately tenanted by Lord Keepers and Lord Chancellors, in which Bacon himself afterwards lived as Lord Chancellor, and which passed after his fall into the hands of the Duke of Buckingham, who has left his mark in the Water Gate which is now seen, far from the river, in the garden of the Thames Embankment. His father was Sir Nicholas Bacon, Elizabeth's first Lord Keeper, the fragment of whose effigy in the Crypt of St. Paul's is one of the few relics of the old Cathedral before the fire. His uncle by marriage was that William Cecil who was to be Lord Burghley. His mother, the sister of Lady Cecil, was one of the daughters of Sir Antony Cook, a person deep in the confidence of the reforming party, who had been tutor of Edward VI. She was a remarkable woman, highly accomplished after the fashion of the ladies of her party, and as would become her father's daughter and the austere and laborious family to which she belonged. She was "exquisitely skilled in the Greek and Latin tongues;" she was passionately religious according to the uncompromising religion which the exiles had brought back with them from Geneva, Strassburg, and Zurich, and which saw in Calvin's theology a solution of all the difficulties, and in his discipline a remedy for all the evils, of mankind. This means that his boyhood from the first was passed among the high places of the world—at one of the greatest crises of English history—in the very centre and focus of its agitations. He was brought up among the chiefs and leaders of the rising religion, in the houses of the greatest and most powerful persons of the State, and naturally, as their child, at times in the Court of the Queen, who joked with him, and called him "her young Lord Keeper." It means also that the religious atmosphere in which he was brought up was that of the nascent and aggressive Puritanism, which was not satisfied with the compromises of the Elizabethan Reformation, and which saw in the moral poverty and incapacity of many of its chiefs a proof against the great traditional system of the Church which Elizabeth was loath to part with, and which, in spite of all its present and inevitable shortcomings, her political sagacity taught her to reverence and trust.

At the age of twelve he was sent to Cambridge, and put under Whitgift at Trinity. It is a question which recurs continually to readers about those times and their

precocious boys, what boys were then? For whatever
was the learning of the universities, these boys took
their place with men and consorted with them, sharing
such knowledge as men had, and performing exercises
and hearing lectures according to the standard of men.
Grotius at eleven was the pupil and companion of
Scaliger and the learned band of Leyden; at fourteen
he was part of the company which went with the
ambassadors of the States-General to Henry IV.; at
sixteen, he was called to the bar, he published an out-
of-the-way Latin writer, Martianus Capella, with a
learned commentary, and he was the correspondent of
De Thou.   When Bacon was hardly sixteen he was
admitted to the Society of "Ancients" of Gray's Inn,
and he went in the household of Sir Amyas Paulet, the
Queen's Ambassador, to France.   He thus spent two
years in France, not in Paris alone, but at Blois, Tours,
and Poitiers.   If this was precocious, there is no indication that it was thought precocious.   It only meant that
clever and promising boys were earlier associated with
men in important business than is customary now.   The
old and the young heads began to work together sooner.
Perhaps they felt that there was less time to spare.
In spite of instances of longevity, life was shorter for
the average of busy men, for the conditions of life were
worse.

Two recollections only have been preserved of his
early years.   One is that, as he told his chaplain, Dr.
Rawley, late in life, he had discovered, as far back as
his Cambridge days, the "unfruitfulness" of Aristotle's
method.   It is easy to make too much of this.   It is
not uncommon for undergraduates to criticise their text-

books : it was the fashion with clever men, as, for
instance, Montaigne, to talk against Aristotle without
knowing anything about him: it is not uncommon for
men who have worked out a great idea to find traces of
it, on precarious grounds, in their boyish thinking. Still,
it is worth noting that Bacon himself believed that his
fundamental quarrel with Aristotle had begun with the
first efforts of thought, and that this is the one recollection remaining of his early tendency in speculation.
The other is more trustworthy, and exhibits that in-
ventiveness which was characteristic of his mind. He
tells us in the *De Augmentis* that when he was in France
he occupied himself with devising an improved system
of cypher-writing—a thing of daily and indispensable
use for rival statesmen and rival intriguers. But the
investigation, with its call on the calculating and com-
bining faculties, would also interest him, as an example
of the discovery of new powers by the human mind.

In the beginning of 1579 Bacon, at eighteen, was
called home by his father's death. This was a great
blow to his prospects. His father had not accomplished what he had intended for him, and Francis
Bacon was left with only a younger son's "narrow
portion." What was worse, he lost one whose credit
would have served him in high places. He entered
on life, not as he might have expected, independent
and with court favour on his side, but with his very
livelihood to gain—a competitor at the bottom of
the ladder for patronage and countenance. This great
change in his fortunes told very unfavourably on his
happiness, his usefulness, and, it must be added, on his
character. He accepted it, indeed, manfully, and at

once threw himself into the study of the law as the
profession by which he was to live. But the law,
though it was the only path open to him, was not the
one which suited his genius, or his object in life. To
the last he worked hard and faithfully, but with doubtful reputation as to his success, and certainly against
the grain. And this was not the worst. To make up
for the loss of that start in life of which his father's
untimely death had deprived him, he became, for almost
the rest of his life, the most importunate and most
untiring of suitors.

In 1579 or 1580 Bacon took up his abode at
Gray's Inn, which for a long time was his home. He
went through the various steps of his profession. He
began, what he never discontinued, his earnest and
humble appeals to his relative the great Lord Burghley,
to employ him in the Queen's service, or to put him in
some place of independence : through Lord Burghley's
favour he seems to have been pushed on at his Inn,
where, in 1586, he was a Bencher; and in 1584 he came
into Parliament for Melcombe Regis. He took some
small part in Parliament : but the only record of his
speeches is contained in a surly note of Recorder Fleet-
wood, who writes as an old member might do of a young
one talking nonsense. He sat again for Liverpool in
the year of the Armada (1588), and his name begins to
appear in the proceedings. These early years, we know,
were busy ones. In them Bacon laid the foundation of
his observations and judgments on men and affairs; and
in them the great purpose and work of his life was conceived and shaped. But they are more obscure years
than might have been expected in the case of a man of

Bacon's genius and family, and of such eager and un-
concealed desire to rise and be at work. No doubt he
was often pinched in his means; his health was weak,
and he was delicate and fastidious in his care of it:
plunged in work, he lived very much as a recluse in his
chambers, and was thought to be reserved, and what
those who disliked him called arrogant. But Bacon was
ambitious—ambitious, in the first place, of the Queen's
notice and favour. He was versatile, brilliant, courtly,
besides being his father's son; and considering how
rapidly bold and brilliant men were able to push their
way and take the Queen's favour by storm, it seems
strange that Bacon should have remained fixedly in the
shade. Something must have kept him back. Burghley
was not the man to neglect a useful instrument with
such good will to serve him. But all that Mr. Spedding's
industry and profound interest in the subject has brought
together throws but an uncertain light on Bacon's long
disappointment. Was it the rooted misgiving of a man
of affairs like Burghley at that passionate contempt of
all existing knowledge and that undoubting confidence
in his own power to make men know, as they never had
known, which Bacon was even now professing? Or was
it something soft and over-obsequious in character which
made the uncle, who knew well what men he wanted,
disinclined to encourage and employ the nephew?
Was Francis not hard enough, not narrow enough, too
full of ideas, too much alive to the shakiness of current
doctrines and arguments on religion and policy? Was
he too open to new impressions, made by objections or
rival views? Or did he show signs of wanting backbone
to stand amid difficulties and threatening prospects?

Did Burghley see something in him of the pliability which he could remember as the serviceable quality of his own young days—which suited those days of rapid change, but not days when change was supposed to be over, and when the qualities which were wanted were those which resist and defy it? The only thing that is clear is that Burghley, in spite of Bacon's continual applications, abstained to the last from advancing his fortunes.

Whether employed by government or not, Bacon began at this time to prepare those carefully-written papers on the public affairs of the day, of which he has left a good many. In our day they would have been pamphlets or magazine articles. In his they were circulated in manuscript, and only occasionally printed. The first of any importance is a letter of advice to the Queen, about the year 1585, on the policy to be followed with a view to keeping in check the Roman Catholic interest at home and abroad. It is calm, sagacious, and, according to the fashion of the age, slightly Machiavellian. But the first subject on which Bacon exhibited his characteristic qualities, his appreciation of facts, his balance of thought, and his power, when not personally committed, of standing aloof from the ordinary prejudices and assumptions of men round him, was the religious condition and prospects of the English Church. Bacon had been brought up in a Puritan household of the straitest sect. His mother was an earnest, severe, and intolerant Calvinist, deep in the interests and cause of her party, bitterly resenting all attempts to keep in order its pretensions. She was a masterful woman, claiming to meddle with her brother-in-law's policy, and though a most affectionate

EARLY LIFE. 11

mother she was a woman of violent and ungovernable temper. Her letters to her son Antony, whom she loved passionately, but whom she suspected of keeping dangerous and papistical company, show us the imperious spirit in which she claimed to interfere with her sons; and they show also that in Francis she did not find all the deference which she looked for. Recommending Antony to frequent "the religious exercises of the sincerer sort," she warns him not to follow his brother's advice or example. Antony was advised to use prayer twice a day with his servants. "Your brother," she adds, "is too negligent therein." She is anxious about Antony's health, and warns him not to fall into his brother's ill-ordered habits; "I verily think your brother's weak stomach to digest hath been much caused and confirmed by untimely going to bed, and then musing *nescio quid* when he should sleep, and then in consequent by late rising and long lying in bed; whereby his men are made slothful and himself continueth sickly. But my sons haste not to hearken to their mother's good counsel in time to prevent." It seems clear that Francis Bacon had shown his mother that not only in the care of his health, but in his judgment on religious matters, he meant to go his own way. Mr. Spedding thinks that she must have had much influence on him : it seems more likely that he resented her interference, and that the hard and narrow arrogance which she read into the Gospel produced in him a strong reaction. Bacon was obsequious to the tyranny of power, but he was never inclined to bow to the tyranny of opinion; and the tyranny of Puritan infallibility was the last thing to which he was likely to submit. His mother

would have wished him to sit under Cartwright and
Travers.   The friend of his choice was the Anglican
preacher, Dr. Andrewes, to whom he submitted all his
works, and whom he called his "inquisitor general;"
and he was proud to sign himself the pupil of Whitgift,
and to write for him—the archbishop of whom Lady
Bacon wrote to her son Antony, veiling the dangerous
sentiment in Greek, "that he was the ruin of the church,
for he loved his own glory more than Christ's."

Certainly, in the remarkable paper on *Controversies in
the Church* (1589), Bacon had ceased to feel or to speak as
a Puritan.   The paper is an attempt to compose the con-
troversy by pointing out the mistakes in judgment, in
temper, and in method on both sides.   It is entirely unlike
what a Puritan would have written : it is too moderate,
too tolerant, too neutral, though like most essays of
conciliation it is open to the rejoinder from both sides—
certainly from the Puritan—that it begs the question by
assuming the unimportance of the matters about which
each contended with so much zeal.   It is the confirmation,
but also the complement, and in some ways the correction of Hooker's contemporary view of the quarrel
which was threatening the life of the English Church,
and not even Hooker could be so comprehensive and so
fair.   For Hooker had to defend much that was indefensible : he had to defend a great traditional system,
just convulsed by a most tremendous shock—a shock
and alteration, as Bacon says, "the greatest and most
dangerous that can be in a State," in which old clues and
habits and rules were confused and all but lost ; in which
a frightful amount of personal incapacity and worthless-
ness had, from sheer want of men, risen to the high

places of the Church; and in which force and violence,
sometimes of the most hateful kind, had come to be
accepted as ordinary instruments in the government of
souls. Hooker felt too strongly the unfairness, the folly,
the intolerant aggressiveness, the malignity of his
opponents,—he was too much alive to the wrongs in-
flicted by them on his own side, and to the incredible
absurdity of their arguments,—to do justice to what was
only too real in the charges and complaints of those
opponents. But Bacon came from the very heart of the
Puritan camp. He had seen the inside of Puritanism—
its best as well as its worst side. He witnesses to the
humility, the conscientiousness, the labour, the learning,
the hatred of sin and wrong, of many of its preachers.
He had heard, and heard with sympathy, all that could
be urged against the bishops' administration, and against
a system of legal oppression in the name of the Church.
Where religious elements were so confusedly mixed, and
where each side had apparently so much to urge on behalf
of its claims, he saw the deep mistake of loftily ignoring
facts, and of want of patience and forbearance with those
who were scandalised at abuses, while the abuses, in some
cases monstrous, were tolerated and turned to profit.
Towards the bishops and their policy, though his language is very respectful, for the government was implicated, he is very severe. They punish and restrain, but
they do not themselves mend their ways or supply what
was wanting; and theirs are "*injuriæ potentiorum,*"—"injuries come from them that have the upper hand." But
Hooker himself did not put his finger more truly and more
surely on the real mischief of the Puritan movement:
on the immense outbreak in it of unreasonable party

spirit and visible personal ambition,—"these are the
true successors of Diotrephes and not my lord bishops:"
—on the gradual development of the Puritan theory till
it came at last to claim a supremacy as unquestionable
and intolerant as that of the Papacy: on the servile
affectation of the fashions of Geneva and Strassburg: on
the poverty and foolishness of much of the Puritan teaching—its inability to satisfy the great questions which it
raised in the soul, its unworthy dealing with scripture
—"naked examples, conceited inferences, and forced
allusions, which mine into all certainty of religion"—
"the word, the bread of life, they toss up and down,
they break it not:" on their undervaluing of moral worth,
if it did not speak in their phraseology—"as they censure virtuous men by the names of *civil* and *moral,* so do
they censure men truly and godly wise, who see into the
vanity of their assertions, by the name of *politiques;*
saying that their wisdom is but carnal and savouring of
man's brain." Bacon saw that the Puritans were aiming
at a tyranny, which, if they established it, would be more
comprehensive, more searching, and more cruel than that
of the older systems; but he thought it a remote and
improbable danger, and that they might safely be tolerated for the work they did in education and preaching,
"because the work of exhortation doth chiefly rest upon
these men, and they have a zeal and hate of sin." But he
ends by warning them lest "that be true which one of
their adversaries said, *that they have but two small wants—
knowledge and love.*" One complaint that he makes of
them is a curious instance of the changes of feeling, or at
least of language, on moral subjects. He accuses them
of "having pronounced generally, and without difference,

all untruths unlawful," forgetful of the Egyptian mid-
wives and Rahab, and Solomon, and even of Him "who,
the more to touch the hearts of the disciples with a holy
dalliance, made as though he would have passed Em-
maus." He is thinking of their failure to apply a
principle which was characteristic of his mode of
thought, that even a statement about a virtue like veracity
"hath limit as all things else have:" but it is odd to
find Bacon bringing against the Puritans the converse of
the charge which his age, and Pascal afterwards, brought
against the Jesuits. The essay, besides being a picture
of the times as regards religion, is an example of what
was to be Bacon's characteristic strength and weakness :
his strength, in lifting up a subject, which had been
degraded by mean and wrangling disputations, into a
higher and larger light, and bringing to bear on it great
principles and the results of the best human wisdom and
experience, expressed in weighty and pregnant maxims ;
his weakness, in forgetting, as, in spite of his philosophy,
he so often did, that the grandest major premises need
well-proved and ascertained minors, and that the enuncia-
tion of a principle is not the same thing as the application of it. Doubtless there is truth in his closing
words; but each party would have made the comment
that what he had to prove, and had not proved, was that
by following his counsel they would "love the whole
better than a part."

"Let them not fear . . . the fond calumny of *neutrality :* but
let them know that is true which is said by a wise man, *that
neuters in contentions are either better or worse than either side.*
These things have I in all sincerity and simplicity set down touching the controversies which now trouble the Church of England :
and that without all art and insinuation, and therefore not like to

be grateful to either part. Notwithstanding, I trust what has been
said shall find a correspondence in their minds which are not em-
barked in partiality, and which *love the whole better than a part.*"

Up to this time, though Bacon had showed himself
capable of taking a broad and calm view of questions
which it was the fashion among good men, and men
who were in possession of the popular ear, to treat with
narrowness and heat, there was nothing to disclose his
deeper thoughts—nothing foreshadowed the purpose
which was to fill his life.   He had, indeed, at the age of
twenty-five, written a "youthful" philosophical essay, to
which he gave the pompous title " *Temporis Partus Maxi-
mus,*" "the Greatest Birth of Time."   But he was thirty-
one when we first find an indication of the great idea and
the great projects which were to make his name famous.
This indication is contained in an earnest appeal to Lord
Burghley for some help which should not be illusory.
Its words are distinct and far-reaching ; and they are the
first words from him which tell us what was in his heart.
The letter has the interest to us of the first announcement of a promise which, to ordinary minds, must have
appeared visionary and extravagant, but which was so
splendidly fulfilled ; the first distant sight of that sea of
knowledge which henceforth was opened to mankind,
but on which no man, as he thought, had yet entered.
It contains the famous avowal—"*I have taken all knowledge to be my province*"—made in the confidence born of
long and silent meditations and questionings, but made
in a simple good faith which is as far as possible from
vain boastfulness.

   "MY LORD—With as much confidence as mine own honest and
faithful devotion unto your service and your honourable correspon-

dence unto me and my poor estate can breed in a man, do I commend myself unto your Lordship. I wax now somewhat ancient;
one and thirty years is a great deal of sand in the hour glass. My
health, I thank God, I find confirmed; and I do not fear that action
shall impair it, because I account my ordinary course of study
and meditation to be more painful than most parts of action are.
I ever bare a mind (in some middle place that I could discharge) to
serve her Majesty, not as a man born under Sol, that loveth honour;
nor under Jupiter, that loveth business (for the contemplative
planet carrieth me away wholly); but as a man born under an
excellent sovereign, that deserveth the dedication of all men's
abilities. Besides, I do not find in myself so much self-love, but
that the greater parts of my thoughts are to deserve well (if I be
able) of my friends, and namely of your Lordship; who, being the
Atlas of this commonwealth, the honour of my house, and the
second founder of my poor estate, I am tied by all duties, both of
a good patriot and of an unworthy kinsman, and of an obliged
servant, to employ whatsoever I am to do you service. Again, the
meanness of my estate doth somewhat move me: for, though I
cannot accuse myself that I am either prodigal or slothful, yet my
health is not to spend, nor my course to get. Lastly, I confess
that I have as vast contemplative ends, as I have moderate civil
ends: for I have taken all knowledge to be my province; and if
I could purge it of two sorts of rovers, whereof the one with frivolous disputations, confutations, and verbosities, the other with
blind experiments and auricular traditions and impostures, hath
committed so many spoils, I hope I should bring in industrious
observations, grounded conclusions, and profitable inventions and
discoveries; the best state of that province. This, whether it be
curiosity or vain glory, or nature, or (if one take it favourably),
philanthropia, is so fixed in my mind as it cannot be removed.
And I do easily see, that place of any reasonable countenance doth
bring commandment of more wits than of a man's own; which is the
thing I greatly affect. And for your Lordship, perhaps you shall
not find more strength and less encounter in any other. And if
your Lordship shall find now, or at any time, that I do seek or affect
any place whereunto any that is nearer unto your Lordship shall
be concurrent, say then that I am a most dishonest man. And if
your Lordship will not carry me on, I will not do as Anaxagoras

did, who reduced himself with contemplation unto voluntary
poverty, but this I will do—I will sell the inheritance I have,
and purchase some lease of quick revenue, or some office of gain
that shall be executed by deputy, and so give over all care of
service, and become some sorry book-maker, or a true pioner in that
mine of truth, which (he said) lay so deep.   This which I have
writ unto your Lordship is rather thoughts than words, being set
down without all art, disguising, or reservation.   Wherein I have
done honour both to your Lordship's wisdom, in judging that that
will be best believed of your Lordship which is truest, and to your
Lordship's good nature, in retaining nothing from you.   And even so
I wish your Lordship all happiness, and to myself means and
occasions to be added to my faithful desire to do you service.   From
my lodgings at Gray's Inn."

This letter, to his unsympathetic and suspicious, but
probably not unfriendly relative, is the key to Bacon's
plan of life; which, with numberless changes of form,
he followed to the end.   That is, a profession, steadily,
seriously, and laboriously kept to, in order to provide
the means of living; and beyond that, as the ultimate
and real end of his life, the pursuit, in a way un-
attempted before, of all possible human knowledge, and
of the methods to improve it and make it sure and fruitful.   And so his life was carried out.   On the one hand,
it was a continual and pertinacious seeking after government employment, which could give credit to his name
and put money in his pocket—attempts by general
behaviour, by professional services when the occasion
offered, by putting his original and fertile pen at the
service of the government, to win confidence, and to
overcome the manifest indisposition of those in power
to think that a man who cherished the chimera of
universal knowledge could be a useful public servant.
On the other hand, all the while, in the crises of his

disappointment or triumph, the one great subject lay
next his heart, filling him with fire and passion—
how really to know, and to teach men to know indeed, and to use their knowledge so as to command
nature; the great hope to be the reformer and re-
storer of knowledge in a more wonderful sense than the
world had yet seen in the reformation of learning and
religion, and in the spread of civilised order in the great
states of the Renaissance time. To this he gave his
best and deepest thoughts; for this he was for ever
accumulating, and for ever rearranging and reshaping
those masses of observation and inquiry and invention
and mental criticism which were to come in as parts
of the great design which he had seen in the visions
of his imagination, and of which at last he was only
able to leave noble fragments, incomplete after numberless recastings. This was not indeed the only, but it
was the predominant and governing interest of his life.
Whether as solicitor for Court favour or public office;
whether drudging at the work of the law, or managing State prosecutions; whether writing an oppor-
tune pamphlet against Spain or Father Parsons, or in-
venting a "device" for his Inn or for Lord Essex to give
amusement to Queen Elizabeth; whether fulfilling his
duties as member of Parliament or rising step by step
to the highest places in the Council Board and the State;
whether in the pride of success or under the amazement
of unexpected and irreparable overthrow, while it
seemed as if he was only measuring his strength against
the rival ambitions of the day, in the same spirit and
with the same object as his competitors, the true motive
of all his eagerness and all his labours was not theirs.

He wanted to be powerful, and still more to be rich : but
he wanted to be so, because without power and without
money he could not follow what was to him the only
thing worth following on earth—a real knowledge of
the amazing and hitherto almost unknown world in
which he had to live. Bacon, to us, at least, at this
distance, who can only judge him from partial and imperfect knowledge, often seems to fall far short of what
a man should be.   He was not one of the high-minded
and proud searchers after knowledge and truth, like
Descartes, who were content to accept a frugal independence so that their time and their thoughts might be their
own. Bacon was a man of the world, and wished to live
in and with the world.   He threatened sometimes retirement, but never with any very serious intention.   In the
Court was his element, and there were his hopes.
Often there seems little to distinguish him from the
ordinary place-hunters, obsequious and selfish, of every
age ; little to distinguish him from the servile and insincere flatterers, of whom he himself complains, who
crowded the antechambers of the great Queen, content to
submit with smiling face and thankful words to the insolence of her waywardness and temper, in the hope, more
often disappointed than not, of hitting her taste on
some lucky occasion, and being rewarded for the accident
by a place of gain or honour.   Bacon's history, as read
in his letters, is not an agreeable one ; after every
allowance made for the fashions of language, and the
necessities of a suitor, there is too much of insincere
profession of disinterestedness, too much of exaggerated
profession of admiration and devoted service, too much
of disparagement and insinuation against others, for a

man who respected himself. He submitted too much to
the miserable conditions of rising which he found. But,
nevertheless it must be said that it was for no mean object, for no mere private selfishness or vanity, that he en-
dured all this. He strove hard to be a great man and a
rich man. But it was that he might have his hands free
and strong and well furnished to carry forward the double
task of overthrowing ignorance and building up the new
and solid knowledge on which his heart was set : that
immense conquest of nature on behalf of man which he
believed to be possible, and of which he believed himself to have the key.

The letter to Lord Burghley did not help him much.
He received the reversion of a place, the Clerkship of the
Council, which did not become vacant for twenty years.
But these years of service declined and place withheld were
busy and useful ones. What he was most intent upon, and
what occupied his deepest and most serious thought, was
unknown to the world round him, and probably not very
intelligible to his few intimate friends, such as his brother
Antony and Dr. Andrewes. Meanwhile he placed his pen
at the disposal of the authorities, and though they regarded
him more as a man of study than of practice and experience, they were glad to make use of it. His versatile genius
found another employment. Besides his affluence in
topics, he had the liveliest fancy and most active imagination. But that he wanted the sense of poetic fitness and
melody, he might almost be supposed, with his reach and
play of thought, to have been capable, as is maintained
in some eccentric modern theories, of writing Shakespeare's plays. No man ever had a more imaginative
power of illustration, drawn from the most remote and

most unlikely analogies; analogies often of the quaintest
and most unexpected kind, but often also not only felicitous in application but profound and true. His powers
were early called upon for some of those sportive compositions in which that age delighted on occasions of
rejoicing or festival. Three of his contributions to these
"devices" have been preserved: two of them composed
in honour of the Queen, as "triumphs," offered by Lord
Essex, one probably in 1592 and another in 1595; a
third for a Gray's Inn revel in 1594. The "devices"
themselves were of the common type of the time, extravagant, odd, full of awkward allegory and absurd
flattery, and running to a prolixity which must make
modern lovers of amusement wonder at the patience of
those days; but the "discourses" furnished by Bacon
are full of fine observation and brilliant thought and wit
and happy illustration, which, fantastic as the general
conception is, raises them far above the level of such
fugitive trifles.

Among the fragmentary papers belonging to this time
which have come down, not the least curious are those
which throw light on his manner of working. While he
was following out the great ideas which were to be the
basis of his philosophy, he was as busy and as painstaking
in fashioning the instruments by which they were to be
expressed; and in these papers we have the records and
specimens of this preparation. He was a great collector
of sentences, proverbs, quotations, sayings, illustrations,
anecdotes, and he seems to have read sometimes, simply
to gather phrases and apt words. He jots down at
random any good and pointed remark which comes into
his thought or his memory; at another time he groups

a set of stock quotations with a special drift, bearing
on some subject, such as the faults of universities or
the habits of lawyers. Nothing is too minute for his
notice. He brings together in great profusion mere
forms, varied turns of expression, heads and tails of
clauses and paragraphs, transitions, connections; he notes
down fashions of compliment, of excuse or repartee,
even morning and evening salutations; he records
neat and convenient opening and concluding sentences,
ways of speaking more adapted than others to give a
special colour or direction to what the speaker or writer
has to say—all that hook-and-eye work, which seems so
trivial and passes so unnoticed as a matter of course, and
which yet is often hard to reach, and which makes all the
difference between tameness and liveliness, between clearness and obscurity—all the difference, not merely to the
ease and naturalness, but often to the logical force of
speech. These collections it was his way to sift and tran-
scribe again and again, adding as well as omitting. From
one of these, belonging to 1594 and the following years,
the *Promus of Formularies and Elegancies*, Mr. Spedding has
given curious extracts; and the whole collection has been
recently edited by Mrs. Henry Pott. Thus it was that he
prepared himself for what, as we read it, or as his audience heard it, seems the suggestion or recollection of the
moment. Bacon was always much more careful of the
value or aptness of a thought than of its appearing new
and original. Of all great writers he least minds repeating himself, perhaps in the very same words; so that a
simile, an illustration, a quotation pleases him, he returns
to it—he is never tired of it; it obviously gives him satisfaction to introduce it again and again. These collections

of odds and ends illustrate another point in his literary
habits. His was a mind keenly sensitive to all analogies
and affinities, impatient of a strict and rigid logical groove,
but spreading as it were tentacles on all sides in quest of
chance prey, and quickened into a whole system of imagination by the electric quiver imparted by a single word,
at once the key and symbol of the thinking it had led to.
And so he puts down word or phrase, so enigmatical to us
who see it by itself, which to him would wake up a whole
train of ideas, as he remembered the occasion of it—how
at a certain time and place this word set the whole moving,
seemed to breathe new life and shed new light, and has
remained the token, meaningless in itself, which reminds
him of so much.

When we come to read his letters, his speeches, his
works, we come continually on the results and proofs of
this early labour. Some of the most memorable and
familiar passages of his writings are to be traced from
the storehouses which he filled in these years of preparation. An example of this correspondence between the
note-book and the composition is to be seen in a paper
belonging to this period, written apparently to form part
of a masque, or as he himself calls it, a "Conference of
Pleasure," and entitled the *Praise of Knowledge.* It is
interesting because it is the first draught which we have
from him of some of the leading ideas and most characteristic language about the defects and the improvement
of knowledge, which were afterwards embodied in the
Advancement and the *Novum Organum.* The whole spirit
and aim of his great reform is summed up in the following fine passage :—

"Facility to believe, impatience to doubt, temerity to assever, glory to know, doubt to contradict, end to gain, sloth to search, seeking things in words, resting in a part of nature,—these and the like have been the things which have forbidden the happy match between the mind of man and the nature of things, and in place thereof have married it to vain notions and blind experiments. . . . Therefore, no doubt, the *sovereignty of man* lieth hid in knowledge : wherein many things are reserved which kings with their treasures cannot buy nor with their force command ; their spials and intelli- gencers can give no news of them ; their seamen and discoverers cannot sail where they grow. Now we govern nature in opinions, but we are thrall unto her in necessity ; but if we could be led by her in invention, we should command her in action."

To the same occasion as the discourse on the *Praise of Knowledge* belongs, also, one in *Praise of the Queen.* As one is an early specimen of his manner of writing on philosophy, so this is a specimen of what was equally characteristic of him—his political and historical writing. It is, in form, necessarily a panegyric, as high-flown and adulatory as such performances in those days were bound to be. But it is not only flattery. It fixes with true discrimination on the points in Elizabeth's character and reign which were really subjects of admira- tion and homage. Thus of her unquailing spirit at the time of the Spanish invasion :—

"Lastly, see a Queen, that when her realm was to have been invaded by an army the preparation whereof was like the travail of an elephant, the provisions infinite, the setting forth whereof was the terror and wonder of Europe ; it was not seen that her cheer, her fashion, her ordinary manner, was anything altered ; not a cloud of that storm did appear in that countenance wherein peace doth ever shine ; but with excellent assurance and advised security she inspired her council, animated her nobility, re- doubled the courage of her people ; still having this noble apprehension, not only that she would communicate her for- tune with them, but that it was she that would protect them, and

not they her; which she testified by no less demonstration than
her presence in camp. Therefore that magnanimity that neither
feareth greatness of alteration, nor the vows of conspirators, nor
the power of the enemy, is more than heroical."

These papers, though he put his best workmanship
into them, as he invariably did with whatever he
touched, were of an ornamental kind. But he did more
serious work. In the year 1592 a pamphlet had been
published on the Continent in Latin and English, *Re-
sponsio ad Edictum Reginæ Angliæ*, with reference to the
severe legislation which followed on the Armada, making
such charges against the Queen and the Government as it
was natural for the Roman Catholic party to make, and
making them with the utmost virulence and unscrupu-
lousness. It was supposed to be written by the ablest
of the Roman pamphleteers, Father Parsons. The
Government felt it to be a dangerous indictment; and
Bacon was chosen to write the answer to it. He had
additional interest in the matter, for the pamphlet made
a special and bitter attack on Burghley, as the person
mainly responsible for the Queen's policy. Bacon's
reply is long and elaborate, taking up every charge, and
reviewing from his own point of view the whole course
of the struggle between the Queen and the supporters
of the Roman Catholic interest abroad and at home. It
cannot be considered an impartial review; besides that
it was written to order, no man in England could then
write impartially in that quarrel; but it is not more
one-sided and uncandid than the pamphlet which it
answers, and Bacon is able to recriminate with effect,
and to show gross credulity and looseness of assertion
on the part of the Roman Catholic advocate. But reli-

gion had too much to do with the politics of both sides
for either to be able to come into the dispute with clean
hands : the Roman Catholics meant much more than
toleration, and the sanguinary punishments of the
English law against priests and Jesuits were edged
by something even keener than the fear of treason.
But the paper contains some large surveys of public
affairs, which probably no one at that time could write
but Bacon. Bacon never liked to waste anything good
which he had written; and much of what he had written
in the panegyric in *Praise of the Queen* is made use
of again, and transferred with little change to the pages
of the *Observations on a Libel*.

CHAPTER II.

BACON AND ELIZABETH.

THE last decade of the century, and almost of Elizabeth's reign (1590 - 1600), was an eventful one to Bacon's fortunes. In it the vision of his great design disclosed itself more and more to his imagination and hopes, and with more and more irresistible fascination. In it he made his first literary venture, the first edition of his *Essays* (1597), ten in number, the first - fruits of his early and ever watchful observation of men and affairs. These years, too, saw his first steps in public life, the first efforts to bring him into importance, the first great trials and tests of his character. They saw the beginning and they saw the end of his relations with the only friend who, at that time, recognised his genius and his purposes, certainly the only friend who ever pushed his claims; they saw the growth of a friendship which was to have so tragical a close, and they saw the beginnings and causes of a bitter personal rivalry which was to last through life, and which was to be a potent element hereafter in Bacon's ruin. The friend was the Earl of Essex. The competitor was the ablest, and also the most truculent and unscrupulous of English lawyers, Edward Coke.

While Bacon, in the shade, had been laying the
foundations of his philosophy of nature, and vainly suing
for legal or political employment, another man had
been steadily rising in the Queen's favour and carrying
all before him at Court, Robert Devereux, Lord Essex ;
and with Essex Bacon had formed an acquaintance which
had ripened into an intimate and affectionate friendship.
We commonly think of Essex as a vain and insolent
favourite, who did ill the greatest work given him to do
—the reduction of Ireland; who did it ill from some un-
explained reason of spite and mischief ; and who, when
called to account for it, broke out into senseless and idle
rebellion.   This was the end : but he was not always thus.
He began life with great gifts and noble ends : he was a
serious, modest, and large-minded student both of books
and things ; and he turned his studies to full account.
He had imagination and love of enterprise, which
gave him an insight into Bacon's ideas such as none of
Bacon's contemporaries had.   He was a man of simple
and earnest religion ; he sympathised most with the
Puritans, because they were serious and because they
were hardly used.   Those who most condemn him
acknowledge his nobleness and generosity of nature.
Bacon in after days, when all was over between them,
spoke of him as a man always *patientissimus veri ;* "the
more plainly and frankly you shall deal with my lord,"
he writes elsewhere, "not only in disclosing particulars,
but in giving him *caveats* and admonishing him of any
error which in this action he may commit (such is his
lordship's nature), the better he will take it."   "He
must have seemed," says Mr. Spedding, a little too
grandly, "in the eyes of Bacon like the hope of the

world." The two men, certainly, became warmly attached. Their friendship came to be one of the closest
kind, full of mutual services, and of genuine affection
on both sides. It was not the relation of a great patron
and useful dependant; it was, what might be expected
in the two men, that of affectionate equality. Each man
was equally capable of seeing what the other was, and
saw it. What Essex's feelings were towards Bacon the
results showed. Bacon, in after years, repeatedly claimed
to have devoted his whole time and labour to Essex's
service. Holding him, he says, to be "the fittest instrument to do good to the State, I applied myself to him in
a manner which I think rarely happeneth among men;
neglecting the Queen's service, mine own fortune, and, in
a sort, my vocation, I did nothing but advise and rumin-
ate with myself . . . anything that might concern his lordship's honour, fortune, or service." The claim is far too
wide. The "Queen's service" had hardly as yet come
much in Bacon's way, and he never neglected it when it
did come, nor his own fortune or vocation: his letters
remain to attest his care in these respects. But, no
doubt, Bacon was then as ready to be of use to Essex,
the one man who seemed to understand and value him,
as Essex was desirous to be of use to Bacon.

And it seemed as if Essex would have the ability as
well as the wish. Essex was, without exception, the
most brilliant man who ever appeared at Elizabeth's
Court, and it seemed as if he were going to be the most
powerful. Leicester was dead. Burghley was growing
old, and indisposed for the adventures and levity which,
with all her grand power of ruling, Elizabeth loved. She
needed a favourite, and Essex was unfortunately marked

out for what she wanted. He had Leicester's fascination
without his mean and cruel selfishness. He was as
generous, as gallant, as quick to descry all great things
in art and life, as Philip Sidney, with more vigour and
fitness for active life than Sidney. He had not Raleigh's
sad, dark depths of thought, but he had a daring courage
equal to Raleigh's, without Raleigh's cynical contempt
for mercy and honour. He had every personal advantage requisite for a time when intellect and ready wit,
and high-tempered valour, and personal beauty, and
skill in affairs, with equal skill in amusements, were expected to go together in the accomplished courtier.
And Essex was a man not merely to be courted and
admired, to shine and dazzle, but to be loved. Elizabeth, with her strange and perverse emotional constitution, loved him, if she ever loved any one. Every one
who served him loved him : and he was as much as any
one could be in those days, a popular favourite. Under
better fortune he might have risen to a great height of
character : in Elizabeth's Court he was fated to be
ruined.

For in that Court all the qualities in him which needed
control received daily stimulus, and his ardour and
high-aiming temper turned into impatience and restless
irritability. He had a mistress who was at one time in
the humour to be treated as a tender woman, at another
as an outrageous flirt, at another as the haughtiest and
most imperious of queens : her mood varied, no one
could tell how, and it was most dangerous to mistake it.
It was part of her pleasure to find in her favourite a
spirit as high, a humour as contradictory and determined,
as her own : it was the charming contrast to the obsequi

ousness or the prudence of the rest; but no one could
be sure at what unlooked-for moment, and how fiercely,
she might resent in earnest a display of what she had
herself encouraged. Essex was ruined for all real greatness by having to suit himself to this bewildering and
most unwholesome and degrading waywardness. She
taught him to think himself irresistible in opinion and
in claims: she amused herself in teaching him how
completely he was mistaken. Alternately spoiled and
crossed, he learned to be exacting, unreasonable, absurd
in his pettish resentments or brooding sullenness. He
learned to think that she must be dealt with by the
same methods which she herself employed. The effect
was not produced in a moment; it was the result of a
courtiership of sixteen years. But it ended in corrupting
a noble nature. Essex came to believe that she who
cowed others must be frightened herself: that the sting-
ing injustice which led a proud man to expect, only to
see how he would behave when refused, deserved to be
brought to reason by a counter-buffet as rough as her
own insolent caprice. He drifted into discontent, into
disaffection, into neglect of duty, into questionable
schemings for the future of a reign that must shortly
end, into criminal methods of guarding himself, of
humbling his rivals and regaining influence. A "fatal
impatience," as Bacon calls it, gave his rivals an advantage which, perhaps in self-defence, they could not fail to
take; and that career, so brilliant, so full of promise of
good, ended in misery, in dishonour, in remorse, on the
scaffold of the Tower.

With this attractive and powerful person Bacon's
fortunes, in the last years of the century, became more

and more knit up. Bacon was now past thirty, Essex
a few years younger. In spite of Bacon's apparent
advantage and interest at Court, in spite of abilities,
which, though his genius was not yet known, his contemporaries clearly recognised, he was still a struggling
and unsuccessful man : ambitious to rise, for no unworthy
reasons, but needy, in weak health, with careless and
expensive habits, and embarrassed with debt. He had
hoped to rise by the favour of the Queen, and for the
sake of his father. For some ill-explained reason he was
to the last disappointed. Though she used him "for
matters of state and revenue," she either did not like
him, or did not see in him the servant she wanted to
advance. He went on to the last pressing his uncle, Lord
Burghley : he applied in the humblest terms, he made
himself useful with his pen, he got his mother to write for
him ; but Lord Burghley, probably because he thought
his nephew more of a man of letters, than a sound lawyer
and practical public servant, did not care to bring him
forward. From his cousin, Robert Cecil, Bacon received
polite words and friendly assurances ; Cecil may have
undervalued him, or have been jealous of him, or suspected him as a friend of Essex : he certainly gave Bacon
good reason to think that his words meant nothing.
Except Essex, and perhaps his brother Antony—the most
affectionate and devoted of brothers—no one had yet
recognised all that Bacon was. Meanwhile time was
passing. The vastness, the difficulties, the attractions
of that conquest of all knowledge which he dreamed of,
were becoming greater every day to his thoughts. The
law, without which he could not live, took up time and
brought in little. Attendance on the Court was ex-

D

pensive, yet indispensable, if he wished for place. His
mother was never very friendly, and thought him
absurd and extravagant. Debts increased and creditors
grumbled. The outlook was discouraging, when his
friendship with Essex opened to him a more hopeful
prospect.

In the year 1593 the Attorney-General's place was
vacant, and Essex, who in that year became a Privy Councillor, determined that Bacon should be Attorney-General.
Bacon's reputation as a lawyer was overshadowed by his
philosophical and literary pursuits. He was thought
young for the office, and he had not yet served in any
subordinate place. And there was another man, who
was supposed to carry all English law in his head, full
of rude force and endless precedents, hard of heart, and
voluble of tongue, who also wanted it. An Attorney-
General was one who would bring all the resources and
hidden subtleties of English law to the service of the
Crown, and use them with thorough-going and unflinching
resolution against those whom the Crown accused of
treason, sedition, or invasion of the prerogative. It is
no wonder that the Cecils, and the Queen herself, thought
Coke likely to be a more useful public servant than
Bacon : it is certain what Coke himself thought about
it, and what his estimate was of the man whom Essex
was pushing against him. But Essex did not take up
his friend's cause in the lukewarm fashion in which
Burghley had patronised his nephew. There was nothing that Essex pursued with greater pertinacity. He
importuned the Queen. He risked without scruple
offending her. She apparently long shrank from directly
refusing his request. The Cecils were for Coke—the

"*Huddler*," as Bacon calls him, in a letter to Essex; but the appointment was delayed. All through 1593, and until April 1594, the struggle went on.

When Robert Cecil suggested that Essex should be content with the Solicitor's place for Bacon, "praying him to be well advised, for if his Lordship had spoken of that it might have been of easier digestion to the Queen," he turned round on Cecil—

"Digest me no digesting (said the Earl); for the Attorneyship is that I must have for Francis Bacon; and in that I will spend my uttermost credit, friendship, and authority against whomsoever, and that whosoever went about to procure it to others, that it should cost both the mediators and the suitors the setting on before they came by it. And this be you assured of, Sir Robert, quoth the Earl, for now do I fully declare myself; and for your own part, Sir Robert, I do think much and strange both of my Lord your father and you, that can have the mind to seek the preferment of a stranger before so near a kinsman; namely, considering if you weigh in a balance his parts and sufficiency in any respect with those of his competitor, excepting only four poor years of admittance, which Francis Bacon hath more than recompensed with the priority of his reading, in all other respects you shall find no comparison between them."

But the Queen's disgust at some very slight show of independence on Bacon's part in Parliament, unforgiven in spite of repeated apologies, together with the influence of the Cecils and the pressure of so formidable and so useful a man as Coke, turned the scale against Essex. In April 1594, Coke was made Attorney. Coke did not forget the pretender to law, as he would think him, who had dared so long to dispute his claims; and Bacon was deeply wounded. "No man," he thought, "had ever received a more exquisite disgrace," and he spoke of retiring to Cambridge "to spend the rest of his life in his studies and contemplations." But Essex was not discouraged. He next pressed eagerly for the Solicitorship. Again, after much waiting he was foiled. An inferior man was put over Bacon's head. Bacon found that Essex, who could do most things, for some reason could not do this. He himself, too, had pressed his suit with the greatest importunity on the Queen, on Burghley, on Cecil, on every one who could help him; he reminded the Queen how many years ago it was since he first kissed her hand in her service, and ever since had used his wits to please; but it was all in vain. For once he lost patience. He was angry with Essex; the Queen's anger with Essex had, he thought, recoiled on his friend. He was angry with the Queen; she held his long waiting cheap; she played with him and amused herself with delay; he would go abroad, and he "knew her Majesty's nature, that she neither careth though the whole surname of the Bacons travelled, nor of the Cecils neither." He was very angry with Robert Cecil; affecting not to believe them, he tells him stories he has heard of his corrupt and underhand dealing. He writes almost a farewell letter of ceremonious but ambiguous thanks to Lord Burghley, hoping that he would impute any offence that Bacon might have given to the "complexion of a suitor and a tired sea-sick suitor," and speaking despairingly of his future success in the law. The humiliations of what a suitor has to go through torment him: "It is my luck," he writes to Cecil, "still to be akin to such things as I neither like in nature nor would willingly meet with in my course, but yet cannot avoid without show of base timorousness or else of unkind or suspicious

strangeness." And to his friend Fulke Greville, he thus
unburdens himself :—

"SIR—I understand of your pains to have visited me, for which
I thank you. My matter is an endless question. I assure you I
had said *Requiesce anima mea ;* but I now am otherwise put to my
psalter; *Nolite confidere.* I dare go no further. Her Majesty had
by set speech more than once assured me of her intention to call
me to her service, which I could not understand but of the place
I had been named to. And now whether *invidus homo hoc fecit ;*
or whether my matter must be an appendix to my Lord of Essex
suit ; or whether her Majesty, pretending to prove my ability,
meaneth but to take advantage of some errors which, like enough,
at one time or other I may commit ; or what is it ; but her Majesty
is not ready to despatch it. And what though the Master of the
Rolls, and my Lord of Essex, and yourself, and others, think my
case without doubt, yet in the meantime I have a hard condition,
to stand so that whatsoever service I do to her Majesty, it shall be
thought to be but *servitium viscatum,* lime-twigs and fetches to
place myself; and so I shall have envy, not thanks. This is a
course to quench all good spirits, and to corrupt every man's
nature ; which will, I fear, much hurt her Majesty's service in the
end. I have been like a piece of stuff bespoken in the shop ; and
if her Majesty will not take me, it may be the selling by parcels
will be more gainful. For to be, as I told you, like a child following a bird, which when he is nearest flieth away and lighteth a
little before, and then the child after it again, and so *in infinitum,*
I am weary of it; as also of wearying my good friends: of whom,
nevertheless, I hope in one course or other gratefully to deserve.
And so, not forgetting your business, I leave to trouble you with
this idle letter; being but *justa et moderata querimonia ;* for indeed
I do confess, *primus amor* will not easily be cast off. And thus
again I commend me to you."

After one more effort the chase was given up, at least
for the moment; for it was soon resumed. But just now
Bacon felt that all the world was against him. He
would retire " out of the sunshine into the shade." One

friend only encouraged him.   He did more.   He helped
him when Bacon most wanted help, in his straightened
and embarrassed "estate."   Essex, when he could do
nothing more, gave Bacon an estate worth at least
£1800.   Bacon's resolution is recorded in the following
letter :—

" IT MAY PLEASE YOUR GOOD LORDSHIP—I pray God her Majesty's
weighing be not like the weight of a balance ; *gravia deorsum levia
sursum*.   But I am as far from being altered in devotion towards
her, as I am from distrust that she will be altered in opinion towards
me, when she knoweth me better.   For myself, I have lost some
opinion, some time, and some means; this is my account; but then
for opinion, it is a blast that goeth and cometh ; for time, it is
true it goeth and cometh not; but yet I have learned that it may
be redeemed.   For means, I value that most ; and the rather,
*because I am purposed not to follow the practice of the law (if her
Majesty command me in any particular, I shall be ready to do her
willing service)* ; and my reason is only, *because it drinketh too much
time, which I have dedicated to better purposes*.   But even for that
point of estate and means, I partly lean to Thales' opinion, That a
philosopher may be rich if he will.   Thus your Lordship seeth how I
comfort myself ; to the increase whereof I would fain please myself
to believe that to be true which my Lord Treasurer writeth; which
is, that it is more than a philosopher morally can disgest.   But without any such high conceit, I esteem it like the pulling out of an
aching tooth, which, I remember, when I was a child, and had
little philosophy, I was glad of when it was done.   For your
Lordship, I do think myself more beholding to you than to any
man.   And I say, I reckon myself as a *common* (not popular but
common) ; and as much as is lawful to be enclosed of a common, so
much your Lordship shall be sure to have.—Your Lordship's to
obey your honourable commands, more settled than ever."

It may be that, as Bacon afterwards maintained, the
closing sentences of this letter implied a significant reserve of his devotion.   But during the brilliant and
stormy years of Essex's career which followed, Bacon's

relations to him continued unaltered. Essex pressed
Bacon's claims whenever a chance offered. He did his
best to get Bacon a rich wife—the young widow of Sir
Christopher Hatton—but in vain. Instead of Bacon
she accepted Coke, and became famous afterwards in the
great family quarrel, in which Coke and Bacon again
found themselves face to face, and which nearly ruined
Bacon before the time. Bacon worked for Essex when
he was wanted, and gave the advice which a shrewd and
cautious friend would give to a man who, by his success
and increasing pride and self-confidence, was running
into serious dangers, arming against himself deadly foes,
and exposing himself to the chances of fortune. Bacon
was nervous about Essex's capacity for war, a capacity
which perhaps was not proved, even by the most brilliant
exploit of the time, the capture of Cadiz, in which Essex
foreshadowed the heroic but well-calculated audacities
of Nelson and Cochrane, and showed himself as little
able as they to bear the intoxication of success, and to
work in concert with envious and unfriendly associates.
At the end of the year 1596, the year in which Essex
had won such reputation at Cadiz, Bacon wrote him a
letter of advice and remonstrance. It is a lively picture
of the defects and dangers of Essex's behaviour as the
Queen's favourite; and it is a most characteristic and
worldly-wise summary of the ways which Bacon would
have him take, to cure the one and escape the other.
Bacon had, as he says, "good reason to think that the
Earl's fortune comprehended his own." And the letter
may perhaps be taken as an indirect warning to Essex
that Bacon must, at any rate, take care of his own
fortune, if the Earl persisted in dangerous courses.

Bacon shows how he is to remove the impressions, strong in the Queen's mind, of Essex's defects; how he is, by due submissions and stratagems, to catch her humour:

> "But whether I counsel you the best, or for the best, duty bindeth me to offer to you my wishes. I said to your Lordship last time, *Martha, Martha, attendis ad plurima, unum sufficit;* win the Queen: if this be not the beginning, of any other course I see no end."

Bacon gives a series of minute directions how Essex is to disarm the Queen's suspicions, and to neutralise the advantage which his rivals take of them; how he is to remove "the opinion of his nature being *opiniastre* and not rulable;" how, avoiding the faults of Leicester and Hatton, he is, as far as he can, to "allege them for authors and patterns." Especially, he must give up that show of soldier-like distinction, which the Queen so disliked, and take some quiet post at Court. He must not alarm the Queen by seeking popularity; he must take care of his estate; he must get rid of some of his officers; and he must not be disquieted by other favourites.

Bacon wished, as he said afterwards, to see him "with a white staff in his hand, as my Lord of Leicester had," an honour and ornament to the Court in the eyes of the people and foreign ambassadors. But Essex was not fit for the part which Bacon urged upon him, that of an obsequious and vigilant observer of the Queen's moods and humours. As time went on, things became more and more difficult between him and his strange mistress: and there were never wanting men who, like Cecil and Raleigh, for good and bad reasons, feared and hated Essex, and who had the craft and the skill to

make the most of his inexcusable errors. At last he
allowed himself, from ambition, from the spirit of contradiction, from the blind passion for doing what he thought
would show defiance to his enemies, to be tempted into
the Irish campaign of 1599. Bacon at a later time
claimed credit for having foreseen and foretold its issue.
"I did as plainly see his overthrow, chained as it were
by destiny to that journey, as it is possible for any man
to ground a judgment on future contingents." He
warned Essex, so he thought in after years, of the
difficulty of the work; he warned him that he would
leave the Queen in the hands of his enemies: "It
would be ill for her, ill for him, ill for the State." "I
am sure," he adds, "I never in anything in my life
dealt with him in like earnestness by speech, by writing,
and by all the means I could devise." But Bacon's
memory was mistaken. We have his letters. When
Essex went to Ireland, Bacon wrote only in the
language of sanguine hope: so little did he see "overthrow chained by destiny to that journey," that "some
good spirit led his pen to presage to his Lordship
success:" he saw in the enterprise a great occasion of
honour to his friend: he gave prudent counsels, but he
looked forward confidently to Essex being as "fatal a
captain to that war, as Africanus was to the war of Car-
thage." Indeed, however anxious he may have been, he
could not have foreseen Essex's unaccountable and to
this day unintelligible failure. But failure was the end,
from whatever cause; failure, disgraceful and complete.
Then followed wild and guilty but abortive projects for
retrieving his failure, by using his power in Ireland to
make himself formidable to his enemies at Court, and

even to the Queen herself. He intrigued with Tyrone:
he intrigued with James of Scotland: he plunged into
a whirl of angry and baseless projects, which came to
nothing the moment they were discussed How empty
and idle they were was shown by his return against
orders to tell his own story at Nonsuch, and by thus
placing himself alone and undeniably in the wrong, in
the power of the hostile Council. Of course it was not
to be thought of that Cecil should not use his advantage in the game. It was too early, irritated though the
Queen was, to strike the final blow. But it is impossible
not to see, looking back over the miserable history, that
Essex was treated in a way which was certain, sooner
or later, to make him, being what he was, plunge into a
fatal and irretrievable mistake. He was treated as a
cat treats a mouse: he was worried, confined, disgraced,
publicly reprimanded, brought just within verge of the
charge of treason, but not quite, just enough to discredit
and alarm him, but to leave him still a certain amount
of play. He was made to see that the Queen's favour
was not quite hopeless; but that nothing but the most
absolute and unreserved humiliation could recover it.
It was plain to any one who knew Essex that this
treatment would drive Essex to madness. "These same
gradations of yours"—so Bacon represents himself ex-
postulating with the Queen on her caprices—"are fitter
to corrupt than to correct any mind of greatness."
They made Essex desperate; he became frightened for
his life, and he had reason to be so, though not in the
way which he feared. At length came the stupid and
ridiculous outbreak of the 8th of February $\frac{1600}{1601}$, a
plot to seize the palace and raise the city against the

ministers, by the help of a few gentlemen armed only
with their rapiers.   As Bacon himself told the Queen,
"if some base and cruel-minded persons had entered
into such an action, it might have caused much blow
and combustion; but it appeared well that they were
such as knew not how to play the malefactors!"   But
it was sufficient to bring Essex within the doom of
treason.

Essex knew well what the stake was.   He lost it,
and deserved to lose it, little as his enemies deserved to
win it; for they, too, were doing what would have cost
them their heads if Elizabeth had known it,—corresponding, as Essex was accused of doing, with Scotland about
the succession, and possibly with Spain.   But they
were playing cautiously and craftily; he with bungling
passion.   He had been so long accustomed to power and
place, that he could not endure that rivals should keep
him out of it.   They were content to have their own
way, while affecting to be the humblest of servants : he
would be nothing less than a Mayor of the Palace.   He
was guilty of a great public crime, as every man is who
appeals to arms for anything short of the most sacred
cause.   He was bringing into England, which had settled
down into peaceable ways, an imitation of the violent
methods of France and the Guises.   But the crime as
well as the penalty belonged to the age, and crimes
legally said to be against the State mean morally very
different things according to the state of society and
opinion.   It is an unfairness verging on the ridiculous,
when the ground is elaborately laid for keeping up the
impression that Essex was preparing a real treason
against the Queen like that of Norfolk.   It was a treason

of the same sort and order as that for which Northumberland sent Somerset to the block : the treason of being an unsuccessful rival.

Meanwhile Bacon had been getting gradually into the unofficial employ of the Government. He had become one of the "Learned Counsel," lawyers with subordinate and intermittent work, used when wanted, but without patent or salary, and not ranking with the regular law officers. The Government had found him useful in affairs of the revenue, in framing interrogatories for prisoners in the Tower, in drawing up reports of plots against the Queen. He did not in this way earn enough to support himself; but he had thus come to have some degree of access to the Queen, which he represents as being familiar and confidential, though he still perceived, as he says himself, that she did not like him. At the first news of Essex's return to England, Bacon greeted him :—

"My Lord—Conceiving that your Lordship came now up in the person of a good servant to see your sovereign mistress, which kind of compliments are many times *instar magnorum meritorum,* and therefore it would be hard for me to find you, I have committed to this poor paper the humble salutations of him *that is more yours than any man's, and more yours than any man.* To these salutations I add a due and joyful gratulation, confessing that your Lordship, in your last conference with me before your journey, spake not in vain, God making it good, That you trusted we should say *Quis putasset !* Which as it is found true in a happy sense, so I wish you do not find another *Quis putasset* in the manner of taking this so great a service. But I hope it is, as he said, *Nubecula est, cito transibit,* and that your Lordship's wisdom and obsequious circumspection and patience will turn all to the best. So referring all to some time that I may attend you, I commit you to God's best preservation."

But when Essex's conduct in Ireland had to be dealt
with, Bacon's services were called for; and from this time
his relations towards Essex were altered. Every one, no
one better than the Queen herself, knew all that he
owed to Essex. It is strangely illustrative of the time,
that especially as Bacon held so subordinate a position,
he should have been required, and should have been
trusted, to act against his only and most generous benefactor. It is strange, too, that however great his loyalty
to the Queen, however much and sincerely he might condemn his friend's conduct, he should think it possible
to accept the task. He says that he made some remonstrance; and he says, no doubt truly, that during the
first stage of the business he used the ambiguous
position in which he was placed to soften Essex's inevitable punishment, and to bring about a reconciliation
between him and the Queen. But he was required, as
the Queen's lawyer, to set forth in public Essex's offences;
and he admits that he did so "not over tenderly." Yet all
this, even if we have misgivings about it, is intelligible. If
he had declined, he could not, perhaps, have done the service which he assures us that he tried to do to Essex; and
it is certain that he would have had to reckon with the
terrible lady who in her old age still ruled England from
the throne of Henry VIII., and who had certainly no great
love for Bacon himself. She had already shown him in a
much smaller matter what was the forfeit to be paid for
any resistance to her will. All the hopes of his life must
perish; all the grudging and suspicious favours which he
had won with such unremitting toil and patient waiting
would be sacrificed, and he would henceforth live under
the wrath of those who never forgave. And whatever he

did for himself, he believed that he was serving Essex. His scheming imagination and his indefatigable pen were at work. He tried strange indirect methods; he invented a correspondence between his brother and Essex, which was to fall into the Queen's hands in order to soften her wrath and show her Essex's most secret feelings. When the Queen proposed to dine with him at his lodge in Twickenham Park, "though I profess not to be a poet," he "prepared a sonnet tending and alluding to draw on her Majesty's reconcilement to my Lord." It was an awkward thing for one who had been so intimate with Essex to be so deep in the counsels of those who hated him. He complains that many people thought him ungrateful and disloyal to his friend, and that stories circulated to his disadvantage, as if he were poisoning the Queen's ear against Essex. But he might argue fairly enough that, wilful and wrong-headed as Essex had been, it was the best that he could now do for him; and as long as it was only a question of Essex's disgrace and enforced absence from Court, Bacon could not be bound to give up the prospects of his life, indeed, his public duty as a subordinate servant of government, on account of his friend's inexcusable and dangerous follies. Essex did not see it so, and in the subjoined correspondence had the advantage; but Bacon's position, though a higher one might be imagined, where men had been such friends as these two men had been, is quite a defensible one:—

" My Lord—No man can better expound my doings than your Lordship, which maketh me need to say the less. Only I humbly pray you to believe that I aspire to the conscience and commendation first of *bonus civis*, which with us is a good and true servant to the Queen, and next of *bonus vir*, that is an honest man. I desire your

Lordship also to think that though I confess I love some things much better than I love your Lordship, as the Queen's service, her quiet and contentment, her honour, her favour, the good of my country, and the like, yet I love few persons better than yourself, both for gratitude's sake and for your own virtues, which cannot hurt but by accident or abuse. Of which my good affection I was ever ready and am ready to yield testimony by any good offices, but with such reservations as yourself cannot but allow : for as I was ever sorry that your Lordship should fly with waxen wings, doubting Icarus' fortune, so for the growing up of your own feathers, specially ostrich's, or any other save of a bird of prey, no man shall be more glad. And this is the axletree whereupon I have turned and shall turn, which to signify to you, though I think you are of yourself persuaded as much, is the cause of my writing ; and so I commend your Lordship to God's goodness. From Gray's Inn, this 20th day of July, 1600.

" Your Lordship's most humbly,

"FR. BACON."

To this letter Essex returned an answer of dignified reserve, such as Bacon might himself have dictated.

"MR. BACON—I can neither expound nor censure your late actions: being ignorant of all of them, save one ; and having directed my sight inward only, to examine myself. You do pray me to believe that you only aspire to the conscience and commendation of *bonus civis* and *bonus vir ;* and I do faithfully assure you, that while that is your ambition (though your course be active and mine contemplative), yet we shall both *convenire in eodem tertio* and *convenire inter nosipsos.* Your profession of affection and offer of good offices are welcome to me. For answer to them I will say but this, that you have believed I have been kind to you, and you may believe that I cannot be other, either upon humour or my own election. I am a stranger to all poetical conceits, or else I should say somewhat of your poetical example. But this I must say, that I never flew with other wings than desire to merit and confidence in my Sovereign's favour ; and when one of these wings failed me I would light nowhere but at my Sovereign's feet, though she suffered me to be bruised with my fall. And till her Majesty, that knows I was never bird of prey, finds it to agree with her will and her

service that my wings should be imped again, I have committed
myself to the mire. No power but my God's and my Sovereign's
can alter this resolution of

" Your retired friend,

" ESSEX."

But after Essex's mad attempt in the city a new state
of things arose. The inevitable result was a trial for high
treason, a trial of which no one could doubt the purpose
and end. The examination of accomplices revealed
speeches, proposals, projects, not very intelligible to us
in the still imperfectly understood game of intrigue that
was going on among all parties at the end of Elizabeth's
reign, but quite enough to place Essex at the mercy of
the Government and the offended Queen. "The new information," says Mr. Spedding, "had been immediately
communicated to Coke and Bacon." Coke, as Attorney-
General, of course conducted the prosecution; and the
next prominent person on the side of the Crown was not
the Solicitor, or any other regular law officer, but Bacon,
though holding the very subordinate place of one of the
"Learned Counsel."

It does not appear that he thought it strange, that he
showed any pain or reluctance, that he sought to be excused. He took it as a matter of course. The part
assigned to Bacon in the prosecution was as important as
that of Coke : and he played it more skilfully and effec-
tively. Trials in those days were confused affairs, often
passing into a mere wrangle between the judges, lawyers,
and lookers-on, and the prisoner at the bar. It was so
in this case. Coke is said to have blundered in his way
of presenting the evidence, and to have been led away
from the point into an altercation with Essex. Probably

it really did not much matter : but the trial was getting
out of its course and inclining in favour of the prisoner,
till Bacon—Mr. Spedding thinks, out of his regular
turn—stepped forward and retrieved matters. This is
Mr. Spedding's account of what Bacon said and did:—

   " By this time the argument had drifted so far away from the point
that it must have been difficult for a listener to remember what it
was that the prisoners were charged with, or how much of the
charge had been proved. And Coke, who was all this time the sole
speaker on behalf of the Crown, was still following each fresh topic
that rose before him, without the sign of an intention or the inti-
mation of a wish to return to the main question and reform the
broken ranks of his evidence. Luckily he seems to have been now
at a loss what point to take next, and the pause gave Bacon an
opportunity of rising. It can hardly have been in pursuance of
previous arrangements ; for though it was customary in those days
to distribute the evidence into parts and to assign several parts to
several counsel, there had been no appearance as yet of any part
being concluded. It is probable that the course of the trial had
upset previous arrangements and confused the parts. At any rate
so it was, however it came to pass, that when Cecil and Essex had
at last finished their expostulation and parted with charitable
prayers, each that the other might be forgiven, then (says
our reporter) Mr. Bacon entered into a speech much after this
fashion :—
   " ' In speaking of this late and horrible rebellion which hath been
in the eyes and ears of all men, I shall save myself much labour in
opening and enforcing the points thereof, insomuch as I speak not
before a country jury of ignorant men, but before a most honourable
assembly of the greatest Peers of the land, whose wisdoms conceive
far more than my tongue can utter ; yet with your gracious and
honourable favours I will presume, if not for information of your
Honours, yet for the discharge of my duty, to say thus much. No
man can be ignorant, that knows matters of former ages, and all
history makes it plain, that there was never any traitor heard of
that durst directly attempt the seat of his liege prince but he
always coloured his practices with some plausible pretence. For
God hath imprinted such a majesty in the face of a prince that no

                            E

private man dare approach the person of his sovereign with a
traitorous intent.   And therefore they run another side course,
oblique et à latere: some to reform corruptions of the State and
religion ; some to reduce the ancient liberties and customs pretended to be lost and worn out ; some to remove those persons that
being in high places make themselves subject to envy ; but all of
them aim at the overthrow of the State and destruction of the present rulers.   And this likewise is the use of those that work mischief of another quality ; as Cain, that first murderer, took up an
excuse for his fact, shaming to outface it with impudency, thus
the Earl made his colour the severing some great men and councillors from her Majesty's favour, and the fear he stood in of his
pretended enemies lest they should murder him in his house.   Therefore he saith he was compelled to fly into the City for succour and
assistance ; not much unlike Pisistratus, of whom it was so anciently
written how he gashed and wounded himself, and in that sort ran
crying into Athens that his life was sought and like to have been
taken away ; thinking to have moved the people to have pitied
him and taken his part by such counterfeited harm and danger ;
whereas his aim and drift was to take the government of the city
into his hands and alter the form thereof.   With like pretences of
dangers and assaults the Earl of Essex entered the City of London
and passed through the bowels thereof, blanching rumours that he
should have been murdered and that the State was sold ; whereas
he had no such enemies, no such dangers : persuading themselves
that if they could prevail all would have done well.   But now
magna scelera terminantur in hæresin: for you, my Lord, should
know that though princes give their subjects cause of discontent,
though they take away the honours they have heaped upon them,
though they bring them to a lower estate than they raised them
from, yet ought they not to be so forgetful of their allegiance that
they should enter into any undutiful act ; much less upon rebellion,
as you, my Lord, have done.   All whatsoever you have or can say in
answer hereof are but shadows.   And therefore methinks it were
best for you to confess, not to justify.' "

Essex was provoked by Bacon's incredulous sneer
about enemies and dangers—"I call forth Mr. Bacon
against Mr. Bacon," and referred to the letters which

Bacon had written in his name, and in which these dangerous enmities were taken for granted. Bacon, in
answer, repeated what he said so often—"That he had
spent more time in vain in studying how to make the
Earl a good servant to the Queen and State, than he had
done in anything else." Once more Coke got the proceedings into a tangle, and once more Bacon came forward to repair the miscarriage of his leader.

"'I have never yet seen in any case such favour shown to any
prisoner; so many digressions, such delivering of evidence by frac-
tions, and so silly a defence of such great and notorious treasons.
May it please your Grace, you have seen how weakly he hath
shadowed his purpose and how slenderly he hath answered the
objections against him. But, my Lord, I doubt the variety of
matters and the many digressions may minister occasion of forgetfulness, and may have severed the judgments of the Lords; and
therefore I hold it necessary briefly to recite the Judges' opinions.'
    "That being done, he proceeded to this effect :—
    "'Now put the case that the Earl of Essex's intents were, as he
would have it believed, to go only as a suppliant to her Majesty:
Shall their petitions be presented by armed petitioners? This must
needs bring loss of property to the prince. Neither is it any point
of law, as my Lord of Southampton would have it believed, that
condemns them of treason. To take secret counsel, to execute it, to
run together in numbers armed with weapons,—what can be the
excuse? Warned by the Lord Keeper, by a herald, and yet persist!
Will any simple man take this to be less than treason?'
    "The Earl of Essex answered that if he had purposed anything
against others than those his private enemies, he would not have
stirred with so slender a company. Whereunto Mr. Bacon answered :—
    "'It was not the company you carried with you but the assist-
ance you hoped for in the City which you trusted unto. The Duke
of Guise thrust himself into the streets of Paris on the day of the
Barricados in his doublet and hose, attended only with eight gentlemen, and found that help in the city which (thanks be to God) you
failed of here. And what followed? The King was forced to put him-

self into a pilgrim's weeds, and in that disguise to steal away to scape their fury. Even such was my Lord's confidence too, and his pretence the same—an all-hail and a kiss to the City. But the end was treason, as hath been sufficiently proved. But when he had once delivered and engaged himself so far into that which the shallowness of his conceit could not accomplish as he expected, the Queen for her defence taking arms against him, he was glad to yield himself; and thinking to colour his practices, turned his pretexts, and alleged the occasion thereof to proceed from a private quarrel.'

"To this" (adds the reporter) "the Earl answered little. Nor was anything said afterwards by either of the prisoners, either in the thrust-and-parry dialogue with Coke that followed, or when they spoke at large to the question why judgment should not be pronounced, which at all altered the complexion of the case. They were both found guilty and sentence passed in the usual form."

Bacon's legal position was so subordinate a place that there must have been a special reason for his employment. It is difficult to avoid the conclusion that, on the part of the Government, Bacon was thus used for the very reason that he had been the friend of Essex. He was not commonly called upon in such prosecutions. He was not employed by Cecil in the Winchester trials of Raleigh, Grey, and Cobham, three years afterwards, nor in those connected with the Gunpowder Plot. He was called upon now because no one could so much damage Essex; and this last proof of his ready service was required by those whose favour, since Essex had gone hopelessly wrong, he had been diligently seeking. And Bacon acquiesced in the demand, apparently without surprise. No record remains to show that he felt any difficulty in playing his part. He had persuaded himself that his public duty, his duty as a good citizen to the Queen and the commonwealth, demanded of him that he should obey the call to do his best to bring a traitor to punishment.

Public duty has claims on a man as well as friendship, and in many conceivable cases, claims paramount to
those of friendship.   And yet friendship, too, has claims,
at least on a man's memory.   Essex had been a dear
friend, if words could mean anything.   He had done
more than any man had done for Bacon, generously and
nobly, and Bacon had acknowledged it in the amplest
terms.   Only a year before he had written, "I am as
much yours as any man's, and as much yours as any man."
It is not, and it was not, a question of Essex's guilt.   It
may be a question whether the whole matter was not
exaggerated as to its purpose, as it certainly was as to its
real danger and mischief.   We at least know that his
rivals dabbled in intrigue and foolish speeches as well as
he ; that little more than two years afterwards Raleigh
and Grey and Cobham were condemned for treason in
much the same fashion as he was; that Cecil to the end
of his days—with whatever purpose—was a pensioner of
Spain.   The question was not whether Essex was guilty.
The question for Bacon was, whether it was becoming in
him, having been what he had been to Essex, to take a
leading part in proceedings which were to end in his
ruin and death.   He was not a judge.   He was not a
regular law officer like Coke.   His only employment had
been casual and occasional.   He might, most naturally, on
the score of his old friendship, have asked to be excused.
Condemning, as he did, his friend's guilt and folly, he
might have refused to take part in a cause of blood, in
which his best friend must perish.   He might honestly
have given up Essex as incorrigible, and have retired to
stand apart in sorrow and silence while the inevitable
tragedy was played out.   The only answer to this

is, that to have declined would have incurred the
Queen's displeasure : he would have forfeited any
chance of advancement; nay, closely connected as he
had been with Essex, he might have been involved in
his friend's ruin. But inferior men have marred their
fortunes by standing by their friends in not undeserved
trouble, and no one knew better than Bacon what was
worthy and noble in human action. The choice lay before him. He seems hardly to have gone through any
struggle. He persuaded himself that he could not help
himself, under the constraint of his duty to the Queen :
and he did his best to get Essex condemned.

And this was not all. The death of Essex was a
shock to the popularity of Elizabeth greater than anything that had happened in her long reign. Bacon's
name also had come into men's mouths as that of a
time-server, who played fast and loose with Essex and
his enemies, and who, when he had got what he could
from Essex, turned to see what he could get from those
who put him to death. A justification of the whole
affair was felt to be necessary; and Bacon was fixed upon
for the distinction and the dishonour of doing it. No
one could tell the story so well, and it was felt that he
would not shrink from it. Nor did he. In cold blood
he sat down to blacken Essex, using his intimate personal
knowledge of the past to strengthen his statements
against a friend who was in his grave, and for whom
none could answer but Bacon himself. It is a well-
compacted and forcible account of Essex's misdoings, on
which of course the colour of deliberate and dangerous
treason was placed. Much of it, no doubt, was true;
but even of the facts, and much more of the colour, there

was no check to be had, and it is certain that it was an object to the Government to make out the worst. It is characteristic that Bacon records that he did not lose sight of the claims of courtesy, and studiously spoke of "my Lord of Essex" in the draft submitted for correction to the Queen; but she was more unceremonious, and insisted that the "rebel" should be spoken of simply as "Essex."

After a business of this kind, fines and forfeitures flowed in abundantly, and were " usually bestowed on deserving servants or favoured suitors by way of reward ; " and Bacon came in for his share. Out of one of the fines he received £1200. " The Queen hath done something for me," he writes to a friendly creditor, " though not in the proportion I had hoped," and he afterwards asked for something more. It was rather under the value of Essex's gift to him in 1594. But she still refused him all promotion. He was without an official place in the Queen's service, and he never was allowed to have it. It is clear that the "Declaration of the Treason of the Earl of Essex," if it justified the Government, did not remove the odium which had fallen on Bacon. Mr. Spedding says that he can find no signs of it. The proof of it is found in the "Apology" which Bacon found it expedient to write after Elizabeth's death and early in James's reign. He found that the recollection of the way in which he had dealt with his friend hung heavy upon him : men hesitated to trust him in spite of his now recognised ability. Accordingly, he drew up an apology, which he addressed to Lord Mountjoy, the friend, in reality half the accomplice, of Essex, in his wild, ill-defined plan for putting pressure

on Elizabeth. It is a clear, able, of course *ex parte* statement of the doings of the three chief actors, two of whom
could no longer answer for themselves, or correct and
contradict the third. It represents the Queen as implac-
able and cruel, Essex as incorrigibly and outrageously
wilful, proud, and undutiful, Bacon himself as using
every effort and device to appease the Queen's anger
and suspiciousness, and to bring Essex to a wiser and
humbler mind. The picture is indeed a vivid one, and
full of dramatic force, of an unrelenting and merciless
mistress bent on breaking and bowing down to the dust
the haughty spirit of a once - loved but rebellious
favourite, whom, though he has deeply offended, she
yet wishes to bring once more under her yoke ; and of
the calm, keen-witted looker-on, watching the dangerous
game, not without personal interest, but with undis-
turbed presence of mind, and doing his best to avert an
irreparable and fatal breach. How far he honestly did
his best for his misguided friend we can only know from
his own report ; but there is no reason to think that he
did· Essex ill service, though he notices in passing an
allegation that the Queen in one of her angry fits had
charged him with this. But his interest clearly was
to make up the quarrel between the Queen and
Essex. Bacon would have been a greater man with
both of them if he had been able to do so. He had
been too deeply in Essex's intimacy to make his new
position of mediator, with a strong bias on the Queen's
side, quite safe and easy for a man of honourable mind ;
but a cool-judging and prudent man may well have
acted as he represents himself acting without forgetting
what he owed to his friend. Till the last great moment

of trial there is a good deal to be said for Bacon : a man
keenly alive to Essex's faults, with a strong sense of
what he owed to the Queen and the State, and with his
own reasonable chances of rising greatly prejudiced by
Essex's folly. But at length came the crisis which
showed the man, and threw light on all that had passed
before, when he was picked out, out of his regular
place, to be charged with the task of bringing home the
capital charge against Essex. He does not say he
hesitated. He does not say that he asked to be excused
the terrible office. He did not flinch as the minister of
vengeance for those who required that Essex should die.
He did his work, we are told by his admiring biographer,
better than Coke, and repaired the blunders of the
prosecution. He passes over very shortly this part of
the business : "it was laid upon me with the rest of my
fellows ;" yet it is the knot and key of the whole, as
far as his own character is concerned. Bacon had his
public duty : his public duty may have compelled him
to stand apart from Essex. But it was his interest, it was
no part of his public duty, which required him to accept
the task of accuser of his friend, and in his friend's direst
need calmly to drive home a well-directed stroke that
should extinguish chances and hopes, and make his ruin
certain. No one who reads his anxious letters about
preferment and the Queen's favour, about his disappointed hopes, about his straitened means and distress
for money, about his difficulties with his creditors—he
was twice arrested for debt—can doubt that the question
was between his own prospects and his friend ; and that
to his own interest he sacrificed his friend and his own
honour.

CHAPTER III.

BACON'S life was a double one. There was the life of
high thinking, of disinterested aims, of genuine enthusiasm, of genuine desire to delight and benefit mankind,
by opening new paths to wonder and knowledge and
power. And there was the put on and worldly life,
the life of supposed necessities for the provision of
daily bread, the life of ambition and self-seeking, which
he followed, not without interest and satisfaction, but at
bottom because he thought he must—must be a great
man, must be rich, must live in the favour of the great,
because without it his great designs could not be
accomplished. His original plan of life was disclosed
in his letter to Lord Burghley : to get some office with
an assured income and not much work, and then to
devote the best of his time to his own subjects. But
this, if it was really his plan, was gradually changed :
first, because he could not get such a place ; and next
because his connection with Essex, the efforts to gain
him the Attorney's place, and the use which the Queen
made of him after Essex could do no more for him,
drew him more and more into public work, and specially
the career of the law. We know that he would not by

preference have chosen the law, and did not feel that his
vocation lay that way. But it was the only way open
to him for mending his fortunes. And so the two lives
went on side by side, the worldly one—he would have
said, the practical one—often interfering with the life
of thought and discovery, and partly obscuring it, but
yet always leaving it paramount in his own mind. His
dearest and most cherished ideas, the thoughts with
which he was most at home and happiest, his deepest
and truest ambitions, were those of an enthusiastic and
romantic believer in a great discovery just within his
grasp. They were such as the dreams and visions of
his great Franciscan namesake, and of the imaginative
seekers after knowledge in the middle ages, real or mythical, Albert the Great, Cornelius Agrippa, Dr. Faustus ;
they were the eager undoubting hopes of the physical
students in Italy and England in his own time, Giordano Bruno, Telesio, Campanella, Gilbert, Galileo, or
the founders of the Italian prototype of "Solomon's
House " in the *New Atlantis*, the precursor of our Royal
Societies, the Academy of the *Lincei* at Rome. Among
these meditations was his inner life. But however he
may have originally planned his course, and though at times
under the influence of disappointment he threatened to retire to Cambridge or to travel abroad, he had bound himself fast to public life, and soon ceased to think of quitting
it. And he had a real taste for it, for its shows, its prizes,
for the laws and turns of the game, for its debates and
vicissitudes. He was no mere idealist or recluse to
undervalue or despise the real grandeur of the world.
He took the keenest interest in the nature and ways of
mankind ; he liked to observe, to generalise in shrewd

and sometimes cynical epigrams. He liked to apply his
powerful and fertile intellect to the practical problems
of society and government, to their curious anomalies,
to their paradoxical phenomena; he liked to address
himself, either as an expounder or a reformer, to the
principles and entanglements of English law; he aspired,
both as a lecturer and a legislator, to improve and
simplify it. It was not beyond his hopes to shape a
policy, to improve administration, to become powerful
by bringing his sagacity and largeness of thought to the
service of the State, in reconciling conflicting forces, in
mediating between jealous parties and dangerous claims.
And he liked to enter into the humours of a Court; to
devote his brilliant imagination and affluence of invention either to devising a pageant which should throw
all others into the shade, or a compromise which should
get great persons out of some difficulty of temper or
pique.

In all these things he was as industrious, as laborious,
as calmly persevering and tenacious, as he was in his
pursuit of his philosophical speculations. He was a com-
pound of the most adventurous and most diversified
ambition, with a placid and patient temper, such as we
commonly associate with moderate desires and the love of
retirement and an easy life. To imagine and dare anything, and never to let go the object of his pursuit, is one
side of him; on the other, he is obsequiously desirous to
please and fearful of giving offence, the humblest and
most grateful and also the most importunate of suitors,
ready to bide his time with an even cheerfulness of spirit,
which yet it was not safe to provoke by ill offices and
the wish to thwart him. He never misses a chance of

proffering his services : he never lets pass an opportunity
of recommending himself to those who could help him.
He is so bent on natural knowledge that we have a sense
of incongruity when we see him engaging in politics as
if he had no other interest. He throws himself with
such zest into the language of the moralist, the theo-
logian, the historian, that we forget we have before us
the author of a new departure in physical inquiry, and
the unwearied compiler of tables of natural history.
When he is a lawyer, he seems only a lawyer. If he had
not been the author of the *Instauratio*, his life would not
have looked very different from that of any other of the
shrewd and supple lawyers who hung on to the Tudor
and Stuart Courts, and who unscrupulously pushed their
way to preferment. He claimed to be, in spite of the
misgivings of Elizabeth and her ministers, as devoted to
public work and as capable of it as any of them. He
was ready for anything, for any amount of business,
ready, as in everything, to take infinite trouble about it.
The law, if he did not like it, was yet no by-work with
him ; he was as truly ambitious as the men with whom
he maintained so keen and for long so unsuccessful a
rivalry. He felt bitterly the disappointment of seeing
men like Coke and Fleming and Doddridge and Hobart
pass before him ; he could not, if he had been only a
lawyer, have coveted more eagerly the places, refused to
him, which they got ; only, he had besides a whole train
of purposes, an inner and supreme ambition, of which
they knew nothing. And with all this, there is no
apparent consciousness of these manifold and varied
interests. He never affected to conceal from himself his
superiority to other men in his aims and in the grasp of

his intelligence. But there is no trace that he prided himself on the variety and versatility of these powers, or that he even distinctly realised to himself that it was anything remarkable that he should have so many dissimilar objects and be able so readily to pursue them in such different directions.

It is doubtful whether, as long as Elizabeth lived, Bacon could ever have risen above his position among the "Learned Counsel," an office without patent or salary or regular employment. She used him, and he was willing to be used; but he plainly did not appear in her eyes to be the kind of man who would suit her in the more prominent posts of her Government. Unusual and original ability is apt, till it is generally recognised, to carry with it suspicion and mistrust, as to its being really all that it seems to be. Perhaps she thought of the possibility of his flying out unexpectedly at some inconvenient pinch, and attempting to serve her interests, not in her way, but in his own; perhaps she distrusted in business and state affairs so brilliant a discourser, whose heart was known, first and above all, to be set on great dreams of knowledge; perhaps those interviews with her in which he describes the counsels which he laid before her, and in which his shrewdness and foresight are conspicuous, may not have been so welcome to her as he imagined; perhaps, it is not impossible, that he may have been too compliant for her capricious taste, and too visibly anxious to please. Perhaps, too, she could not forget, in spite of what had happened, that he had been the friend, and not the very generous friend, of Essex. But, except as to a share of the forfeitures, with which he was not satisfied, his fortunes did not rise under Elizabeth.

Whatever may have been the Queen's feelings towards
him, there is no doubt that one powerful influence, which
lasted into the reign of James, was steadily adverse
to his advancement. Burghley had been strangely
niggardly in what he did to help his brilliant nephew ;
he was going off the scene, and probably did not care to
trouble himself about a younger and uncongenial aspirant
to service. But his place was taken by his son, Robert
Cecil ; and Cecil might naturally have been expected to
welcome the co-operation of one of his own family, who
was foremost among the rising men of Cecil's own generation, and who certainly was most desirous to do him service. But it is plain that he early made up his mind to keep
Bacon in the background. It is easy to imagine reasons,
though the apparent shortsightedness of the policy may
surprise us ; but Cecil was too reticent and self-controlled
a man to let his reasons appear, and his words, in answer
to his cousin's applications for his assistance, were always
kind, encouraging, and vague. But we must judge by
the event, and that makes it clear that Cecil did not
care to see Bacon in high position. Nothing can account for Bacon's strange failure for so long a time to
reach his due place in the public service but the secret
hostility, whatever may have been the cause, of Cecil.

There was also another difficulty. Coke was the great
lawyer of the day, a man whom the Government could
not dispense with, and whom it was dangerous to offend.
And Coke thoroughly disliked Bacon. He thought
lightly of his law, and he despised his refinement and his
passion for knowledge. He cannot but have resented
the impertinence, as he must have thought it, of Bacon
having been for a whole year his rival for office. It is

possible that if people then agreed with Mr. Spedding's
opinion as to the management of Essex's trial, he may
have been irritated by jealousy ; but a couple of months
after the trial (April 29, 1601) Bacon sent to Cecil, with
a letter of complaint, the following account of a scene in
Court between Coke and himself :—

" *A true remembrance of the abuse I received of Mr. Attorney-General
publicly in the Exchequer the first day of term; for the truth
whereof I refer myself to all that were present.*

"I moved to have a reseizure of the lands of Geo. Moore, a re-
lapsed recusant, a fugitive and a practising traytor ; and showed
better matter for the Queen against the discharge by plea, which is
ever with a *salvo jure.* And this I did in as gentle and reasonable
terms as might be.

"Mr. Attorney kindled at it, and said, '*Mr. Bacon, if you have
any tooth against me pluck it out ; for it will do you more hurt than
all the teeth in your head will do you good.*' I answered coldly in
these very words : '*Mr. Attorney, I respect you; I fear you not;
and the less you speak of your own greatness, the more I will think
of it.*'

"He replied, '*I think scorn to stand upon terms of greatness towards
you, who are less than little ; less than the least;*' and other such
strange light terms he gave me, with that insulting which cannot
be expressed.

"Herewith stirred, yet I said no more but this : '*Mr. Attorney,
do not depress me so far ; for I have been your better, and may be
again, when it please the Queen.*'

"With this he spake, neither I nor himself could tell what, as
if he had been born Attorney-General ; and in the end bade me not
meddle with the Queen's business, but with mine own ; and that I
was unsworn, etc. I told him, sworn or unsworn was all one to
an honest man ; and that I ever set my service first, and myself
second ; and wished to God that he would do the like.

"Then he said, it were good to clap a *cap. ultegatum* upon my
back ! To which I only said he could not ; and that he was at fault,
for he hunted upon an old scent. He gave me a number of dis-

graceful words besides ; which I answered with silence, and showing
that I was not moved with them."

The threat of the *capias ultegatum* was probably in
reference to the arrest of Bacon for debt in September
1593. After this, we are not surprised at Bacon writing
to Coke, "who take to yourself a liberty to disgrace and
disable my law, my experience, my discretion," that,
" since I missed the Solicitor's place (the rather I think
by your means) I cannot expect that you and I shall ever
serve as Attorney and Solicitor together, but either serve
with another on your remove, or step into some other
course." And Coke, no doubt, took care that it should
be so. Cecil, too, may possibly have thought that Bacon
gave no proof of his fitness for affairs in thus bringing
before him a squabble in which both parties lost their
tempers.

Bacon was not behind the rest of the world in "the
posting of men of good quality towards the King ;" in the
rush which followed the Queen's death, of those who were
eager to proffer their services to James, for whose peaceful accession Cecil had so skilfully prepared the way.
He wrote to every one who, he thought, could help him :
to Cecil, and to Cecil's man—" I pray you, as you find
time let him know that he is the personage in the State
which I love most ; " to Northumberland, " If I may be
of any use to your Lordship, by my head, tongue, pen,
means, or friends, I humbly pray you to hold me your
own ; " to the King's Scotch friends and servants, even to
Southampton, the friend of Essex, who had been shut up
in the Tower since his condemnation with Essex, and
who was now released. "This great change," Bacon
assured him, "hath wrought in me no other change

F

towards your Lordship than this, that I may safely be now
that which I truly was before." Bacon found in after
years that Southampton was not so easily conciliated.
But at present Bacon was hopeful: "In mine own particular," he writes, "I have many comforts and assurances; but in mine own opinion the chief is, that the
*canvassing world is gone, and the deserving world is
come."* He asks to be recommended to the King—"I
commend myself to your love and to the well-using of
my name, as well in repressing and answering for me,
if there be any biting or nibbling at it in that place, as
in impressing a good conceit and opinion of me, chiefly
in the King, as otherwise in that Court." His pen had
been used under the government of the Queen, and he
had offered a draft of a proclamation to the King's
advisers. But though he obtained an interview with the
King, James's arrival in England brought no immediate
prospect of improvement in Bacon's fortunes. Indeed, his
name was at first inadvertently passed over in the list of
Queen's servants who were to retain their places. The
first thing we hear of is his arrest a second time for
debt, and his letters of thanks to Cecil, who had rendered
him assistance, are written in deep depression.

"For my purpose or course, I desire to meddle as little as I can
in the King's causes, his Majesty now abounding in counsel; and to
follow my private thrift and practice, and to marry with some convenient advancement. For as for any ambition, I do assure your
Honour, mine is quenched. In the Queen's, my excellent Mistress's,
time the *quorum* was small : her service was a kind of freehold, and
it was a more solemn time. All those points agreed with my nature
and judgement. My ambition now I shall only put upon my pen,
whereby I shall be able to maintain memory and merit of the times
succeeding.

" Lastly, for this divulged and almost prostituted title of knighthood, I could without charge, by your Honour's mean, be content
to have it, both because of this late disgrace and because I have
three new knights in my mess in Gray's Inn's commons ; and because
I have found out an alderman's daughter, an handsome maiden, to
my liking."

Cecil, however, seems to have required that the money
should be repaid by the day ; and Bacon only makes a
humble request, which, it might be supposed, could have
been easily granted.

" IT MAY PLEASE YOUR GOOD LORDSHIP—In answer of your
last letter, your money shall be ready before your day : principal, interest, and costs of suit. So the sheriff promised, when
I released errors ; and a Jew takes no more. The rest cannot
be forgotten, for I cannot forget your Lordship's *dum memor ipse
mei :* and if there have been *aliquid nimis*, it shall be amended.
And, to be plain with your Lordship, that will quicken me now
which slackened me before. Then I thought you might have had
more use of me than now I suppose you are like to have. Not but
I think the impediment will be rather in my mind than in the matter
or times. But to do you service I will come out of my religion at
any time.

" For my knighthood, I wish the manner might be such as might
grace me, since the matter will not ; I mean, that I might not be
merely gregarious in a troop. The coronation is at hand. It may
please your Lordship to let me hear from you speedily. So I continue your Lordship's ever much bounden,

" FR. BACON.

" From Gorhambury, this 16th of July 1603."

But it was not done. He " obtained his title, but
not in a manner to distinguish him. He was knighted
at Whitehall two days before the coronation, but had to
share the honour with 300 others."

It was not quite true that his " ambition was
quenched." For the rest of Cecil's life Cecil was the

first man at James's Court; and to the last there was
one thing that Bacon would not appear to believe—he
did not choose to believe that it was Cecil who kept
him back from employment and honour. To the last
he persisted in assuming that Cecil was the person
who would help, if he could, a kinsman devoted to his
interests and profoundly conscious of his worth.   To
the last he commended his cause to Cecil in terms of
unstinted affection and confiding hope.   It is difficult
to judge of the sincerity of such language.   The mere
customary language of compliment employed by every
one at this time was of a kind which to us sounds intolerable.   It seems as if nothing that ingenuity could
devise was too extravagant for an honest man to use,
and for a man who respected himself to accept.   It
must not, indeed, be forgotten that conventionalities, as
well as insincerity, differ in their forms in different
times; and that insincerity may lurk behind frank and
clear words, when they are the fashion, as much as in
what is like mere fulsome adulation.   But words mean
something, in spite of forms and fashions.   When a
man of great genius writes his private letters, we wish
generally to believe on the whole what he says; and there
are no limits to the esteem, the honour, the confidence,
which Bacon continued to the end to express towards
Cecil.   Bacon appeared to trust him—appeared, in spite
of continued disappointments, to rely on his goodwill
and good offices.   But for one reason or another Bacon
still remained in the shade.   He was left to employ his
time as he would, and to work his way by himself.

He was not idle.   He prepared papers which he meant
should come before the King, on the pressing subjects of

the day. The Hampton Court conference between the
Bishops and the Puritan leaders was at hand, and he
drew up a moderating paper on the *Pacification of the
Church.* The feeling against him for his conduct towards Essex had not died away, and he addressed to
Lord Mountjoy that *Apology concerning the Earl of
Essex,* so full of interest, so skilfully and forcibly
written, so vivid a picture of the Queen's ways with
her servants, which has every merit except that of
clearing Bacon from the charge of disloyalty to his
best friend. The various questions arising out of the
relations of the two kingdoms, now united under James,
were presenting themselves. They were not of easy
solution, and great mischief would follow if they were
solved wrongly. Bacon turned his attention to them.
He addressed a discourse to the King on the union of
the two kingdoms, the first of a series of discussions on
the subject which Bacon made peculiarly his own, and
which, no doubt, first drew the King's attention and
favour to him.

But for the first year of James's reign he was
unnoticed by the King, and he was able to give his
attention more freely to the great thought and hope of
his life. This time of neglect gave him the opportunity
of leisurely calling together and examining the ideas
which had long had hold of his mind about the state of
human knowledge, about the possibilities of extending
it, about the hopes and powers which that new knowledge opened, and about the methods of realising this
great prospect. This, the passion of his life, never
asleep even in the hottest days of business, or the
most hopeless days of defeat, must have had full play

during these days of suspended public employment. He
was a man who was not easily satisfied with his attempts
to arrange the order and proportions of his plans for
mastering that new world of unknown truth, which
he held to be within the grasp of man, if he would only
dare to seize it; and he was much given to vary the
shape of his work, and to try experiments in composition
and even style. He wrote and rewrote. Besides what
was finally published, there remains a larger quantity of
work which never reached the stage of publication. He
repeated over and over again the same thoughts, the
same images and characteristic sayings. Among these
papers is one which sums up his convictions about the
work before him, and the vocation to which he had been
called in respect of it. It is in the form of a "Proem"
to a treatise on the *Interpretation of Nature*. It was never
used in his published works; but, as Mr. Spedding says,
it has a peculiar value as an authentic statement of what
he looked upon as his special business in life. It is
this mission which he states to himself in the following
paper. It is drawn up in "stately Latin." Mr.
Spedding's translation is no unworthy representation of
the words of the great Prophet of Knowledge :—

"Believing that I was born for the service of mankind, and
regarding the care of the Commonwealth as a kind of common
property which, like the air and water, belongs to everybody, I set
myself to consider in what way mankind might be best served, and
what service I was myself best fitted by nature to perform.

"Now among all the benefits that could be conferred upon
mankind, I found none so great as the discovery of new arts,
endowments, and commodities for the bettering of man's life. . . .
But if a man could succeed, not in striking out some particular
invention, however useful, but in kindling a light in nature—a

light that should in its very rising touch and illuminate all the
border regions that confine upon the circle of our present knowledge ;
and so spreading further and further should presently disclose and
bring into sight all that is most hidden and secret in the world, —
that man (I thought) would be the benefactor indeed of the human
race, — the propagator of man's empire over the universe, the
champion of liberty, the conqueror and subduer of necessities.

"For myself, I found that I was fitted for nothing so well as
for the study of Truth ; as having a mind nimble and versatile
enough to catch the resemblances of things (which is the chief
point), and at the same time steady enough to fix and distinguish
their subtler differences ; as being gifted by nature with desire to
seek, patience to doubt, fondness to meditate, slowness to assert,
readiness to reconsider, carefulness to dispose and set in order ; and
as being a man that neither affects what is new nor admires what
is old, and that hates every kind of imposture. So I thought my
nature had a kind of familiarity and relationship with Truth.

"Nevertheless, because my birth and education had seasoned
me in business of State ; and because opinions (so young as I was)
would sometimes stagger me ; and because I thought that a man's
own country has some special claims upon him more than the rest
of the world ; and because I hoped that, if I rose to any place of
honour in the State, I should have a larger command of industry
and ability to help me in my work ;—for these reasons I both
applied myself to acquire the arts of civil life, and commended my
service, so far as in modesty and honesty I might, to the favour of
such friends as had any influence. In which also I had another
motive : for I felt that those things I have spoken of—be they great
or small—reach no further than the condition and culture of this
mortal life ; and I was not without hope (the condition of religion
being at that time not very prosperous) that if I came to hold office
in the State, I might get something done too for the good of men's
souls. When I found, however, that my zeal was mistaken for
ambition, and my life had already reached the turning-point, and
my breaking health reminded me how ill I could afford to be so
slow, and I reflected moreover that in leaving undone the good that
I could do by myself alone, and applying myself to that which
could not be done without the help and consent of others, I was by
no means discharging the duty that lay upon me,—I put all those

thoughts aside, and (in pursuance of my old determination) betook
myself wholly to this work.   Nor am I discouraged from it because
I see signs in the times of the decline and overthrow of that knowledge and erudition which is now in use.   Not that I apprehend
any more barbarian invasions (unless possibly the Spanish empire
should recover its strength, and having crushed other nations by
arms should itself sink under its own weight): but the civil wars
which may be expected, I think (judging from certain fashions
which have come in of late), to spread through many countries—
together with the malignity of sects, and those compendious arti-
fices and devices which have crept into the place of solid
erudition — seem to portend for literature and the sciences a
tempest not less fatal, and one against which the Printing office
will be no effectual security.   And no doubt but that fair-weather
learning which is nursed by leisure, blossoms under reward and
praise, which cannot withstand the shock of opinion, and is liable
to be abused by tricks and quackery, will sink under such impedi-
ments as these.   Far otherwise is it with that knowledge, whose
dignity is maintained by works of utility and power.   For the
injuries, therefore, which should proceed from the times, I am not
afraid of them ; and for the injuries which proceed from men, I am
not concerned.   For if any one charge me with seeking to be wise
over-much, I answer simply that modesty and civil respect are fit
for civil matters ; in contemplations nothing is to be respected but
Truth.   If any one call on me for *works*, and that presently ; I tell
him frankly, without any imposture at all, that for me—a man
not old, of weak health, my hands full of civil business, entering
without guide or light upon an argument of all others the most
obscure, — I hold it enough to have constructed the machine, though
I may not succeed in setting it on work. . . . If, again, any one ask
me, not indeed for actual works, yet for definite promises and fore-
casts of the works that are to be, I would have him know that the
knowledge which we now possess will not teach a man even what
to *wish*.   Lastly—though this is a matter of less moment—if any
of our politicians, who use to make their calculations and con-
jectures according to persons and precedents, must needs interpose
his judgment in a thing of this nature, I would but remind him
how (according to the ancient fable) the lame man keeping the
course won the race of the swift man who left it ; and that there is

no thought to be taken about precedents, for the thing is without precedent.

"For myself, my heart is not set upon any of those things which depend upon external accidents. I am not hunting for fame : I have no desire to found a sect, after the fashion of heresiarchs ; and to look for any private gain from such an undertaking as this, I count both ridiculous and base. Enough for me the consciousness of well-deserving, and those real and effectual results with which Fortune itself cannot interfere."

In 1604 James's first Parliament met, and with it Bacon returned to an industrious public life, which was not to be interrupted till it finally came to an end with his strange and irretrievable fall. The opportunity had come ; and Bacon, patient, vigilant, and conscious of great powers and indefatigable energy, fully aware of all the conditions of the time, pushed at once to the front in the House of Commons. He lost no time in showing that he meant to make himself felt. The House of Commons had no sooner met than it was involved in a contest with the Chancery, with the Lords, and finally with the King himself, about its privileges—in this case, its exclusive right to judge of the returns of its members. Bacon's time was come for showing the King both that he was willing to do him service, and that he was worth being employed. He took a leading part in the discussions, and was trusted by the House as their spokesman and reporter in the various conferences. The King, in his overweening confidence in his absolute prerogative, had, indeed, got himself into serious difficulty ; for the privilege was one which it was impossible for the Commons to give up. But Bacon led the House to agree to an arrangement which saved their rights ; and under a cloud of words of extravagant flattery, he put the King in

good humour, and elicited from him the spontaneous
proposal of a compromise which ended a very dangerous
dispute. " The King's voice," said Bacon, in his report
to the House, " was the voice of God in man, the good
spirit of God in the mouth of man : I do not say the
voice of God, and not of man : I am not one of Herod's
flatterers : a curse fell upon him that said it, a curse on
him that suffered it. We might say, as was said to
Solomon, We are glad O King that we give account to
you, because you discern what is spoken."

The course of this Parliament, in which Bacon was
active and prominent, showed the King, probably for the
first time, what Bacon was. The session was not so
stormy as some of the later ones ; but occasions arose
which revealed to the King and to the House of Commons the deeply discordant assumptions and purposes by
which each party was influenced, and which brought out
Bacon's powers of adjusting difficulties and harmonising
claims. He never wavered in his loyalty to his own
House, where it is clear that his authority was great.
But there was no limit to the submission and reverence
which he expressed to the King, and, indeed, to his
desire to bring about what the King desired, as far as it
could be safely done. Dealing with the Commons, his
policy was " to be content with the substance and not to
stand on the form." Dealing with the King, he was
forward to recognise all that James wanted recognised
of his kingcraft and his absolute sovereignty. Bacon
assailed with a force and keenness, which showed what he
could do as an opponent, the amazing and intolerable
grievances arising out of the survival of such feudal customs as Wardship and Purveyance ; customs which made

over a man's eldest son and property, during a minority, to the keeping of the King, that is, to a King's favourite, and allowed the King's servants to cut down a man's timber before the windows of his house. But he urged that these grievances should be taken away with the utmost tenderness for the King's honour and the King's purse. In the great and troublesome questions relating to the Union he took care to be fully prepared. He was equally strong on points of certain and substantial importance, equally quick to suggest accommodations where nothing substantial was touched. His attitude was one of friendly and respectful independence. It was not misunderstood by the King. Bacon, who had hitherto been an unsworn and unpaid member of the Learned Counsel, now received his office by patent, with a small salary, and he was charged with the grave business of preparing the work for the Commissioners for the Union of the Kingdoms, in which, when the Commission met, he took a foremost and successful part.

But the Parliament before which their report was to be laid did not meet till ten months after the work of the Commission was done (Dec. 1604—Nov. 1605). For nearly another year Bacon had no public work. The leisure was used for his own objects. He was interested in history in a degree only second to his interest in nature; indeed, but for the engrossing claims of his philosophy of nature, he might have been the first and one of the greatest of our historians. He addressed a letter to the Chancellor Ellesmere on the deficiencies of British history, and on the opportunities which offered for supplying them. He himself could at present do nothing; "but because there be so many good painters, both for hand

and colours, it needeth but encouragement and instructions to give life and light unto it." But he mistook, in
this as in other instances, the way in which such things
are done. Men do not accomplish such things to order,
but because their souls compel them, as he himself was
building up his great philosophical structure, in the midst
of his ambition and disappointment. And this interval
of quiet enabled him to bring out his first public appeal
on the subject which most filled his mind. He completed in English the *Two Books of the Advancement of
Knowledge*, which were published at a book shop at the
gateway of Gray's Inn in Holborn (Oct. 1605). He intended that it should be published in Latin also; but he
was dissatisfied with the ornate translation sent him from
Cambridge, and probably he was in a hurry to get the book
out. It was dedicated to the King, not merely by way
of compliment, but with the serious hope that his interest
might be awakened in the subjects which were nearest
Bacon's heart. Like other of Bacon's hopes, it was disappointed. The King's studies and the King's humours
were not of the kind to make him care for Bacon's visions
of the future, or his eager desire to begin at once a novel
method of investigating the facts and laws of nature;
and the appeal to him fell dead. Bacon sent the book
about to his friends with explanatorv letters. To Sir
T. Bodley he writes:—

"I think no man may more truly say with the Psalm, *Multum
incola fuit anima mea* [Ps. 120] than myself. For I do confess since
I was of any understanding, my mind hath in effect been absent
from that I have done; and in absence are many errors which I
willingly acknowledge: and among them, this great one which led
the rest; that knowing myself by inward calling to be fitter to
hold a book than to play a part, I have led my life in civil causes,

for which I was not very fit by nature, and more unfit by the pre-
occupation of my mind. Therefore, calling myself home, I have
now enjoyed myself; whereof likewise I desire to make the world
partaker."

To Lord Salisbury, in a note of elaborate compliment,
he describes his purpose by an image which he repeats
more than once. "I shall content myself to awake
better spirits, *like a bell-ringer, which is first up to call
others to church.*" But the two friends whose judgment
he chiefly valued, and who, as on other occasions, were
taken into his most intimate literary confidence, were
Bishop Andrewes, his "inquisitor," and Toby Matthews,
a son of the Archbishop of York, who had become a
Roman Catholic, and lived in Italy, seeing a good deal
of learned men there, apparently the most trusted of all
Bacon's friends.

When Parliament met again in November 1605, the
Gunpowder Plot and its consequences filled all minds.
Bacon was not employed about it by Government, and
his work in the House was confined to carrying on
matters left unfinished from the previous session. On
the rumour of legal promotions and vacancies Bacon once
more applied to Salisbury for the Solicitorship (March
1606). But no changes were made, and Bacon was "still
next the door." In May 1606 he did what had for some
time been in his thoughts: he married; not the lady
whom Essex had tried to win for him, that Lady Hatton
who became the wife of his rival Coke, but one whom
Salisbury helped him to gain, an alderman's daughter,
Alice Barnham, "an handsome maiden," with some money
and a disagreeable mother, by her second marriage, Lady
Packington. Bacon's curious love of pomp amused the

gossips of the day. " Sir Francis Bacon," writes Carleton
to Chamberlain, "was married yesterday to his young
wench, in Maribone Chapel. He was clad from top to
toe in purple, and hath made himself and his wife such
store of raiments of cloth of silver and gold that it draws
deep into her portion." Of his married life we hear next
to nothing : in his *Essay on Marriage*, he is not enthusiastic in its praise ; almost the only thing we know is that
in his will, twenty years afterwards, he showed his dissatisfaction with his wife, who after his death married
again. But it gave him an additional reason, and an
additional plea, for pressing for preferment : and in the
summer of 1606 the opening came. Coke was made
Chief-Justice of the Common Pleas, leaving the Attorney's
place vacant. A favourite of Salisbury's, Hobart, became
Attorney, and Bacon hoped for some arrangement by
which the Solicitor Doddridge might be otherwise pro-
vided for, and he himself become Solicitor. Hopeful as
he was, and patient of disappointments, and of what other
men would have thought injustice and faithlessness, he
felt keenly both the disgrace and the inconvenience of
so often expecting place, and being so often passed over.
While the question was pending, he wrote to the King,
the Chancellor, and Salisbury. His letter to the King is
a record in his own words of his public services. To the
Chancellor, whom he believed to be his supporter, he
represented the discredit which he suffered—"he was a
common gaze and a speech;" "the little reputation which
by his industry he gathered, being scattered and taken
away by continual disgraces, *every new man coming
above me ;*" and his wife and his wife's friends were
making him feel it. The letters show what Bacon

thought to be his claims, and how hard he found it to
get them recognised.   To the Chancellor he urged,
among other things, that time was slipping by :

"I humbly pray your Lordship to consider that time groweth
precious with me, and that a married man is seven years elder
in his thoughts the first day. . . . And were it not to satisfy my
wife's friends, and to get myself out of being a common gaze and a
speech, I protest before God I would never speak word for it.   But
to conclude, as my honourable Lady your wife was some mean to
make me to change the name of another, so if it please you to help
me to change my own name, I can be but more and more bounden
to you ; and I am much deceived if your Lordship find not the
King well inclined, and my Lord of Salisbury forward and affectionate."

To Salisbury he writes :—

"I may say to your Lordship, in the confidence of your poor
kinsman, and of a man by you advanced, *Tu idem fer opem,
qui spem dedisti ;* for I am sure it was not possible for any living
man to have received from another more significant and com-
fortable words of hope ; your Lordship being pleased to tell me,
during the course of my last service, that you would raise me ;
and that when you had resolved to raise a man, you were more careful of him than himself ; and that what you had done for me in my
marriage was a benefit to me, but of no use to your Lordship. . . .
And I know, and all the world knoweth, that your Lordship is no
dealer of holy water, but noble and real ; and on my part I am of
a sure ground that I have committed nothing that may deserve
alteration.   And therefore my hope is your Lordship will finish a
good work, and consider that time groweth precious with me, and
that I am now *vergentibus annis.*   And although I know your fortune is not to need an hundred such as I am, yet I shall be ever
ready to give you my best and first fruits, and to supply (as much
as in me lieth) worthiness by thankfulness."

Still the powers were deaf to his appeals ; at any rate
he had to be content with another promise.   Consider-

ing the ability which he had shown in Parliament, the
wisdom and zeal with which he had supported the
Government, and the important position which he held
in the House of Commons, the neglect of him is unintelligible, except on two suppositions : that the Government, that is Cecil, were afraid of anything but the mere
routine of law, as represented by such men as Hobart
and Doddridge ; or that Coke's hostility to him was un-
abated, and Coke still too important to be offended.

Bacon returned to work when the Parliament met,
November 1606. The questions arising out of the Union,
the question of naturalisation, its grounds and limits, the
position of Scotchmen born *before* or *since* the King's
accession, the *Antenati* and *Postnati*, the question of a
union of laws, with its consequences, were discussed with
great keenness and much jealous feeling. On the question of naturalisation Bacon took the liberal and larger
view. The immediate union of laws he opposed as
premature. He was a willing servant of the House,
and the House readily made use of him. He reported
the result of conferences, even when his own opinion
was adverse to that of the House. And he reported
the speeches of such persons as Lord Salisbury, probably
throwing into them both form and matter of his own.
At length, "silently, on the 25th of June," 1607, he
was appointed Solicitor-General. He was then forty-
seven.

"It was also probably about this time," writes Mr.
Spedding, "that Bacon finally settled the plan of his
'*Great Instauration*,' and began to call it by that name."

CHAPTER IV.

THE great thinker and idealist, the great seer of a world of knowledge to which the men of his own generation were blind, and which they could not, even with his help, imagine a possible one, had now won the first step in that long and toilsome ascent to success in life, in which for fourteen years he had been baffled. He had made himself, for good and for evil, a servant of the Government of James I. He was prepared to discharge with zeal and care all his duties. He was prepared to perform all the services which that Government might claim from its servants. He had sought, he had passionately pressed to be admitted within that circle in which the will of the King was the supreme law; after that, it would have been ruin to have withdrawn or resisted; but it does not appear that the thought or wish to resist or withdraw ever presented itself; he had thoroughly convinced himself that in doing what the King required he was doing the part of a good citizen and a faithful servant of the State and Commonwealth. The two lives, the two currents of purpose and effort, were still there. Behind all the wrangle of the courts and the devising of questionable legal subtleties to support some

unconstitutional encroachment, or to outflank the defence
of some obnoxious prisoner, the high philosophical meditations still went on ; the remembrance of their sweetness
and grandeur wrung more than once from the jaded
lawyer or the baffled counsellor the complaint, in words
which had a great charm for him, *Multum incola fuit
anima mea*,—" My soul hath long dwelt," where it would
not be. But opinion, and ambition, and the immense
convenience of being great, and rich, and powerful, and
the supposed necessities of his condition, were too strong
even for his longings to be the interpreter and the servant of nature. There is no trace of the faintest reluctance on his part to be the willing minister of a court of
which not only the principal figure, but the arbiter and
governing spirit, was to be George Villiers, Duke of
Buckingham.

The first leisure that Bacon had after he was appointed
Solicitor he used in a characteristic way. He sat down
to make a minute stock-taking of his position and its
circumstances. In the summer of 1608 he devoted a
week of July to this survey of his life, its objects and
its appliances ; and he jotted down, day by day, through
the week, from his present reflections, or he transcribed
from former note-books, a series of notes in loose order,
mostly very rough and not always intelligible, about
everything that could now concern him. This curious
and intimate record, which he called *Commentarius Solutus*,
was discovered by Mr. Spedding, who not unnaturally
had some misgivings about publishing so secret and so
ambiguous a record of a man's most private confidences
with himself. But there it was, and, as it was known,
he no doubt decided wisely in publishing it as it stands ;

he has done his best to make it intelligible, and he has
also done his best to remove any unfavourable impressions that might arise from it.   It is singularly interesting as an evidence of Bacon's way of working, of his
watchfulness, his industry, his care in preparing himself
long beforehand for possible occasions, his readiness to
take any amount of trouble about his present duties, his
self-reliant desire for more important and difficult ones.
It exhibits his habit of self-observation and self-correction,
his care to mend his natural defects of voice, manner,
and delivery; it is even more curious in showing him
watching his own physical constitution and health, in the
most minute details of symptoms and remedies, equally
with a scientific and a practical object.   It contains his
estimate of his income, his expenditure, his debts, sche-
dules of lands and jewels, his rules for the economy of
his estate, his plans for his new gardens, and terraces,
and ponds, and buildings at Gorhambury.   He was now a
rich man, valuing his property at £24,155 and his income at £4975, burdened with a considerable debt, but
not more than he might easily look to wipe out.   But,
besides all these points, there appear the two large interests of his life, the reform of philosophy, and his ideal
of a great national policy.   The "greatness of Britain"
was one of his favourite subjects of meditation.   He
puts down in his notes the outline of what should be
aimed at to secure and increase it; it is to make the
various forces of the great and growing empire work together in harmonious order, without waste, without
jealousy, without encroachment and collision; to unite
not only the interests but the sympathies and aims of
the Crown with those of the people and Parliament; and

so to make Britain, now in peril from nothing but from
the strength of its own discordant elements, that
"Monarchy of the West" in reality, which Spain was in
show, and, as Bacon always maintained, only in show.
The survey of the condition of his philosophical enterprise takes more space.   He notes the stages and points
to which his plans have reached ; he indicates, with a
favourite quotation or apophthegm—"*Plus ultra*"—
"*ausus vana contemnere*"—"*aditus non nisi sub persona
infantis,*" soon to be familiar to the world in his published
writings — the lines of argument, sometimes alternative ones, which were before him ; he draws out schemes
of inquiry, specimen tables, distinctions and classifications about the subject of Motion, in English interlarded
with Latin, or in Latin interlarded with English, of his
characteristic and practical sort ; he notes the various
sources from which he might look for help and co-
operation—"of learned men beyond the seas"—"to
begin first in France to print it "—"laying for a place to
command wits and pens :" he has his eye on rich and
childless bishops, on the enforced idleness of State
prisoners in the Tower, like Northumberland and
Raleigh, on the great schools and universities, where
he might perhaps get hold of some college for "Inventors"—as we should say, for the endowment of research.
These matters fill up a large space of his notes.   But
his thoughts were also busy about his own advancement.
And to these sheets of miscellaneous memoranda Bacon
confided not only his occupations and his philosophical
and political ideas, but, with a curious innocent unre-
serve, the arts and methods which he proposed to use
in order to win the favour of the great and to pull down

the reputation of his rivals.   He puts down in detail
how he is to recommend himself to the King and the
King's favourites :—

"To set on foot and maintain access with his Majesty, Dean
of the Chapel, May, Murray.   Keeping a course of access at the
beginning of every term and vacation, with a memorial.   To attend
some time his repasts, or to fall into a course of familiar discourse.
To find means to win a conceit, not open, but private, of being
affectionate and assured to the Scotch, and fit to succeed Salisbury
in his manage in that kind ; Lord Dunbar, Duke of Lennox, and
Daubiny : secret."

Then, again, of Salisbury :—

"Insinuate myself to become privy to my Lord of Salisbury's
estate."   "To correspond with Salisbury in a habit of natural but
no ways perilous boldness, and in vivacity, invention, care to cast
and enterprise (but with due caution), for this manner I judge
both in his nature freeth the stands, and in his ends pleaseth him
best, and promiseth more use of me.   I judge my standing out, and
not favoured by Northampton, must needs do me good with Salisbury, specially comparative to the Attorney."

The Attorney Hobart filled the place to which Bacon
had so long aspired, and which he thought, perhaps
reasonably, that he could fill much better.   At any rate
one of the points to which he recurs frequently in his
notes, is to exhort himself to make his own service a
continual contrast to the Attorney's ; "to have in mind
and use the Attorney's weakness ;" enumerating a list
of instances.   "Too full of cases and distinctions.
Nibbling solemnly ; he distinguisheth but apprehends
not."   "No gift with his pen in proclamations and the
like," and at last he draws out in a series of epigrams
his view of "Hubbard's disadvantages" :—

"Better at shift than at drift. . . *Subtilitas sine acrimonia.* . .

No power with the judge. . . He will alter a thing but not mend.
. . He puts into patents and deeds words not of law but of common sense and discourse. . . Sociable save in profit. . . He doth
depopulate mine office ; otherwise called inclose. . . I never
knew any one of so good a speech with a worse pen." . .

Then in a marginal note—"Solemn goose. Stately,
leastwise nodd (?) crafty. They have made him believe
that he is wondrous wise." And, finally, he draws up a
paper of counsels and rules for his own conduct,
"*Custumæ aptæ ad Individuum*"—which might supply an
outline for an essay on the arts of behaviour proper for
a rising official ; a sequel to the biting irony of the
essays on *Cunning* and *Wisdom for a Man's Self*.

"To furnish my L. of S. with ornaments for public speeches.
To make him think how he should be reverenced by a Lord
Chancellor, if I were ; Princelike.

"To prepare him for matters to be handled in Council or before
the King aforehand, and to show him and yield him the fruits of
my care.

"To take notes in tables, when I attend the Council, and sometimes to move out of a memorial shewed and seen. To have particular occasions, fit and graceful and continual, to maintain private
speech with every the great persons, and sometimes drawing more
than one together. *Ex imitatione Att.* This specially in public
places, and without care or affectation. At Council table to make
good my L. of Salisb. motions and speeches, and for the rest sometimes one sometimes another ; chiefly his, that is most earnest and
in affection.

"To suppress at once my speaking, with panting and labour of
breath and voice. Not to fall upon the main too sudden, but to
induce and intermingle speech of good fashion. To use at once
upon entrance given of speech, though abrupt, to compose and
draw in myself. To free myself at once from payt. (?) of formality
and compliment, though with some show of carelessness, pride,
and rudeness."

(And then follows a long list of matters of business to be attended to.)

These arts of a court were not new; it was not new for men to observe them in their neighbours and rivals. What was new was the writing them down, with deliberate candour, among a man's private memoranda, as things to be done and with the intention of practising them. This of itself, it has been suggested, shows that they were unfamiliar and uncongenial to Bacon; for a man reminds himself of what he is apt to forget. But a man reminds himself also of what seems to him, at the moment, most important, and what he lays most stress upon. And it is clear that these are the rules, rhetorical and ethical, which Bacon laid down for himself in pursuing the second great object of his life—his official advancement; and that, whatever we think of them, they were the means which he deliberately approved.

As long as Salisbury lived, the distrust which had kept Bacon so long in the shade kept him at a distance from the King's ear, and from influence on his counsels. Salisbury was the one Englishman in whom the King had become accustomed to confide, in his own conscious strangeness to English ways and real dislike and suspicion of them; Salisbury had an authority which no one else had, both from his relations with James at the end of Elizabeth's reign, and as the representative of her policy and the depositary of its traditions; and if he had lived, things might not, perhaps, have been better in James's government, but many things, probably, would have been different. But while Salisbury was supreme, Bacon, though very alert and zealous, was mainly busied with his official work; and the Solicitor's place had become, as he says, a "mean thing" compared with the Attorney's, and also an extremely laborious

place, "one of the painfullest places in the kingdom."
Much of it was routine; but responsible and fatiguing
routine.   But if he was not in Salisbury's confidence, he
was prominent in the House of Commons.   The great
and pressing subject of the time was the increasing
difficulties of the revenue, created partly by the inevitable changes of a growing state, but much more by the
King's incorrigible wastefulness.   It was impossible to
realise completely the great dream and longing of the
Stuart kings and their ministers, to make the Crown
independent of parliamentary supplies; but to dispense
with these supplies as much as possible, and to make as
much as possible of the revenue permanent, was the
continued and fatal policy of the Court.   The "Great
Contract"—a scheme by which, in return for the surren-
der by the Crown of certain burdensome and dangerous
claims of the Prerogative, the Commons were to assure
a large compensating yearly income to the Crown—was
Salisbury's favourite device during the last two years of
his life.   It was not a prosperous one.   The bargain was
an ill-imagined and not very decorous transaction between
the King and his people.   Both parties were naturally
jealous of one another, suspicious of underhand dealing
and tacit changes of terms, prompt to resent and take
offence, and not easy to pacify when they thought
advantage had been taken; and Salisbury, either by his
own fault, or by yielding to the King's canny shiftiness,
gave the business a more haggling and huckstering look
than it need have had.   Bacon, a subordinate of the
Government, but a very important person in the Commons, did his part, loyally, as it seems, and skilfully in
smoothing differences, and keeping awkward questions

from making their appearance. Thus he tried to stave
off the risk of bringing definitely to a point the King's
cherished claim to levy "impositions," or custom duties,
on merchandise, by virtue of his prerogative—a claim
which he warned the Commons not to dispute, and
which Bacon, maintaining it as legal in theory, did his
best to prevent them from discussing, and to persuade
them to be content with restraining. Whatever he
thought of the "Great Contract," he did what was
expected of him in trying to gain for it fair play. But
he made time for other things also. He advised, and
advised soundly, on the plantation and finance of Ireland.
It was a subject in which he took deep interest. A few
years later, with only too sure a foresight, he gave the
warning, "lest Ireland civil become more dangerous to
us than Ireland savage." He advised—not soundly in
point of law, but curiously in accordance with modern
notions—about endowments; though, in this instance,
in the famous will case of Thomas Sutton, the founder
of the Charter House, his argument probably covered
the scheme of a monstrous job in favour of the needy
Court. And his own work went on in spite of the
pressure of the Solicitor's place. To the first years of
his official life belong three very interesting fragments,
intended to find a provisional place in the plan of the
"Great Instauration." To his friend Toby Matthews, at
Florence, he sent in manuscript the great attack on the
old teachers of knowledge, which is perhaps the most
brilliant, and also the most insolently unjust and un-
thinking piece of rhetoric ever composed by him,—the
Redargutio Philosophiarum.

" I send you at this time the only part which hath any harshness;

and yet I framed to myself an opinion, that whosoever allowed well
of that preface which you so much commend, will not dislike, or at
least ought not to dislike, this other speech of preparation; for it
is written out of the same spirit, and out of the same necessity.
Nay it doth more fully lay open that the question between me and
the ancients is not of the virtue of the race, but of the rightness of
the way. And to speak truth, it is to the other but as *palma* to
pugnus, part of the same thing more large. . . . Myself am like
the miller of Huntingdon, that was wont to pray for peace amongst
the willows; for while the winds blew, the wind-mills wrought,
and the water-mill was less customed. So I see that controversies
of religion must hinder the advancement of sciences. Let me conclude with my perpetual wish towards yourself, that the approbation of yourself by your own discreet and temperate carriage, may
restore you to your country, and your friends to your society.
And so I commend you to God's goodness.

"Gray's Inn, this 10th of October 1609."

To Bishop Andrewes he sent, also in manuscript,
another piece, belonging to the same plan—the deeply
impressive treatise called *Visa et Cogitata*—what Francis
Bacon had seen of nature and knowledge, and what he
had come by meditation to think of what he had seen.
The letter is not less interesting than the last, in respect
to the writer's purposes, his manner of writing, and his
relations to his correspondent.

"MY VERY GOOD LORD—Now your Lordship hath been so long
in the church and the palace disputing between kings and popes,
methinks you should take pleasure to look into the field, and re-
fresh your mind with some matter of philosophy; though that
science be now through age waxed a child again, and left to boys
and young men; and because you were wont to make me believe
you took liking to my writings, I send you some of this vacation's
fruits; and thus much more of my mind and purpose. I hasten
not to publish; perishing I would prevent. And I am forced to
respect as well my times as the matter. For with me it is thus,
and I think with all men in my case, if I bind myself to an argu-

ment, it loadeth my mind ; but if I rid my mind of the present cogitation, it is rather a recreation. This hath put me into these miscellanies ; which I purpose to suppress, if God give me leave to write a just and perfect volume of philosophy, which I go on with, though slowly. I send not your Lordship too much, lest it may glut you. Now let me tell you what my desire is. If your Lordship be so good now, as when you were the good Dean of West-minster, my request to you is, that not by pricks, but by notes, you would mark unto me whatsoever shall seem unto you either not current in the style, or harsh to credit and opinion, or inconvenient for the person of the writer ; for no man can be judge and party : and when our minds judge by reflection of ourselves, they are more subject to error. And though for the matter itself my judgement be in some things fixed, and not accessible by any man's judgement that goeth not my way, yet even in those things, the admonition of a friend may make me express myself diversly. I would have come to your Lordship, but that I am hastening to my house in the country. And so I commend your Lordship to God's good-ness."

There was yet another production of this time, of which we have a notice from himself in a letter to Toby Matthews, the curious and ingenious little treatise on the *Wisdom of the Ancients*, " one of the most popular of his works," says Mr. Spedding, " in his own and in the next generation," but of value to us mainly for its quaint poetical colour, and the unexpected turns, like answers to a riddle, given to the ancient fables. When this work was published, it was the third time that he had appeared as an author in print. He thus writes about it and him-self :—

" MR. MATTHEW—I do heartily thank you for your letter of the 24th of August from Salamanca ; and in recompense thereof, I send you a little work of mine that hath begun to pass the world. They tell me my Latin is turned into silver, and become current. Had you been here, you should have been my inquisitor before it came forth ; but I think the greatest inquisitor in Spain will allow

it. . . . My great work goeth forward : and, after my manner, I
alter ever when I add.   So that nothing is finished till all be
finished.

'From Gray's Inn, the 17th of February 1610."

In the autumn of 1611 the Attorney-General was ill,
and Bacon reminded both the King and Salisbury of his
claim.   He was afraid, he writes to the King, with an
odd forgetfulness of the persistency and earnestness of
his applications, " that *by reason of my slowness to sue*, and
apprehend occasions upon the sudden, keeping one plain
course of painful service, I may *in fine dierum* be in
danger to be neglected and forgotten."   The Attorney
recovered ; but Bacon, on New Year's Tide of $16\frac{11}{12}$,
wrote to Salisbury to thank him for his goodwill.   It is
the last letter of Bacon's to Salisbury which has come
down to us.

"IT MAY PLEASE YOUR GOOD LORDSHIP—I would entreat the
new year to answer for the old, in my humble thanks to your Lordship, both for many your favours, and chiefly that upon the occasion of Mr. Attorney's infirmity I found your Lordship even as I
would wish.   This doth increase a desire in me to express my thankful mind to your Lordship ; hoping that though I find age and
decays grow upon me, yet I may have a flash or two of spirit left
to do you service.   And I do protest before God, without compliment or any light vein of mind, that if I knew in what course of
life to do you best service, I would take it, and make my thoughts,
which now fly to many pieces, be reduced to that center.   But all
this is no more than I am, which is not much, but yet the entire
of him that is——"

In the following May (May 24, 1612) Salisbury died.
From this date James passed from government by a
minister, who, whatever may have been his faults, was
laborious, public-spirited, and a statesman, into his own
keeping and into the hands of favourites, who cared only

for themselves. With Cecil ceased the traditions of the
days of Elizabeth and Burghley, in many ways evil and
cruel traditions, but not ignoble and sordid ones ; and
James was left without the stay, and also without the
check, which Cecil's power had been to him. The field
was open for new men and new ways ; the fashions and
ideas of the time had altered during the last ten years,
and those of the Queen's days had gone out of date.
Would the new turn out for the better or the worse ?
Bacon, at any rate, saw the significance of the change
and the critical eventfulness of the moment. It was his
habit of old to send memorials of advice to the heads of
the Government, apparently without such suggestions
seeming more intrusive or officious than a leading article
seems now, and perhaps with much the same effect. It
was now a time to do so, if ever ; and he was in an
official relation to the King which entitled him to proffer
advice. He at once prepared to lay his thoughts before
the King, and to suggest that he could do far better
service than Cecil, and was ready to take his place.
The policy of the "Great Contract" had certainly
broken down, and the King, under Cecil's guidance, had
certainly not known how to manage an English parliament. In writing to the King, he found it hard to
satisfy himself. Several draft letters remain, and it is
not certain which of them, if any, was sent. But
immediately on Salisbury's death he began, May 29th,
a letter in which he said that he had never yet been
able to show his affection to the King, "having been as
a hawk tied to another's fist ; " and if, "as was said to
one that spake great words, *Amice, verba tua desiderant
civitatem,* your Majesty say to me, *Bacon, your words*

require a place to speak them," yet that "place or not place" was with the King. But the draft breaks off abruptly, and with the date of the 31st we have the following :—

"Your Majesty hath lost a great subject and a great servant. But if I should praise him in propriety, I should say that he was a fit man to keep things from growing worse, but no very fit man to reduce things to be much better. For he loved to have the eyes of all Israel a little too much upon himself, and to have all business still under the hammer, and like clay in the hands of the potter, to mould it as he thought good ; so that he was more *in operatione* than *in opere*. And though he had fine passages of action, yet the real conclusions came slowly on. So that although your Majesty hath grave counsellors and worthy persons left, yet you do as it were turn a leaf, wherein if your Majesty shall give a frame and constitution to matters, before you place the persons, in my simple opinion it were not amiss. But the great matter and most instant for the present, is the consideration of a Parliament, for two effects : the one for the supply of your estate, the other for the better knitting of the hearts of your subjects unto your Majesty, according to your infinite merit ; for both which, Parliaments have been and are the antient and honourable remedy.

"Now because I take myself to have a little skill in that region, as one that ever affected that your Majesty mought in all your causes not only prevail, but prevail with satisfaction of the inner man ; and though no man can say but I was a perfect and peremptory royalist, yet every man makes me believe that I was never one hour out of credit with the lower house ; my desire is to know, whether your Majesty will give me leave to meditate and propound unto you some preparative remembrances touching the future Parliament."

Whether he sent this or not, he prepared another draft. What had happened in the meanwhile we know not, but Bacon was in a bitter mood, and the letter reveals, for the first time, what was really in Bacon's heart about the "great subject and great servant," of

whom he had just written so respectfully, and with
whom he had been so closely connected for most of his
life. The fierceness which had been gathering for years
of neglect and hindrance under that placid and patient
exterior broke out. He offered himself as Cecil's successor in business of State. He gave his reason for
being hopeful of success. Cecil's bitterest enemy could
not have given it more bitterly.

"My principal end being to do your Majesty service, I crave
leave to make at this time to your Majesty this most humble oblation of myself. I may truly say with the psalm, *Multum incola
fuit anima mea;* for my life hath been conversant in things
wherein I take little pleasure. Your Majesty may have heard
somewhat that my father was an honest man, and somewhat you
may have seen of myself, though not to make any true judgement
by, because I have hitherto had only *potestatem verborum,* nor that
neither. I was three of my young years bred with an ambassador
in France, and since I have been an old truant in the school-house
of your. council-chamber, though on the second form ; yet longer
than any that now sitteth hath been upon the head form. If your
Majesty find any aptness in me, or if you find any scarcity in others,
whereby you may think it fit for your service to remove me to
business of State ; although I have a fair way before me for profit
(and by your Majesty's grace and favour for honour and advancement), and in a course less exposed to the blasts of fortune, *yet now
that he is gone, quo vivente virtutibus certissimum exitium,* I will
be ready as a chessman to be wherever your Majesty's royal hand
shall set me. Your Majesty will bear me witness, I have not suddenly opened myself thus far. I have looked upon others, I see
the exceptions, I see the distractions, and I fear Tacitus will be a
prophet, *magis alii homines quam alii mores.* I know mine own
heart, and I know not whether God that hath touched my heart
with the affection may not touch your royal heart to discern it.
Howsoever, I shall at least go on honestly in mine ordinary course,
and supply the rest in prayers for you, remaining, etc."

This is no hasty outburst. In a later paper on the

true way of retrieving the disorders of the King's finances,
full of large and wise counsel, after advising the King
not to be impatient, and assuring him that a state of
debt is not so intolerable—"for it is no new thing for
the greatest Kings to be in debt," and all the great men
of the Court had been in debt without any "manner of
diminution of their greatness "—he returns to the charge
in detail against Salisbury and the Great Contract.

"My second prayer is, that your Majesty—in respect of the
hasty freeing of your state—would not descend to any means, or
degree of means, which carrieth not a symmetry with your Majesty and greatness. *He is gone from whom those courses did
wholly flow.* To have your wants and necessities in particular as
it were hanged up in two tablets before the eyes of your lords and
commons, to be talked of for four months together ; To have all
your courses to help yourself in revenue or profit put into printed
books, which were wont to be held *arcana imperii :* To have such
worms of aldermen to lend for ten in the hundred upon good assurance, and with such entreaty (?) as if it should save the bark of your
fortune : To contract still where mought be had the readiest payment, and not the best bargain : To stir a number of projects for
your profit, and then to blast them, and leave your Majesty nothing
but the scandal of them : To pretend even carriage between your
Majesty's rights and the ease of the people, and to satisfy neither :
These courses and others the like I hope are gone with the deviser
of them ; which have turned your Majesty to inestimable prejudice."

And what he thought of saying, but on further consideration struck out, was the following.   It is no wonder that he struck it out, but it shows what he felt
towards Cecil.

"I protest to God, though I be not superstitious, when I saw
your M.'s book against Vorstius and Arminius, and noted your
zeal to deliver the majesty of God from the vain and indign com-
prehensions of heresy and degenerate philosophy, as you had by
your pen formerly endeavoured to deliver kings from the usurpation

of Rome, *perculsit illico animum* that God would set shortly upon
you some visible favour, *and let me not live if I thought not of the
taking away of that man.*"

And from this time onwards he scarcely ever men-
tions Cecil's name in his correspondence with James but
with words of condemnation, which imply that Cecil's
mischievous policy was the result of private ends. Yet
this was the man to whom he had written the "New
Year's Tide" letter six months before ; a letter which is
but an echo to the last of all that he had been accustomed
to write to Cecil, when asking assistance or offering
congratulation. Cecil had, indeed, little claim on Bacon's
gratitude ; he had spoken him fair in public, and no
doubt in secret distrusted and thwarted him. But to
the last Bacon did not choose to acknowledge this. Had
James disclosed something of his dead servant, who left
some strange secrets behind him, which showed his unsuspected hostility to Bacon ? Except on this supposition
(but there is nothing to support it), no exaggeration of
the liberty allowed to the language of compliment is
enough to clear Bacon of an insincerity which is almost
inconceivable in any but the meanest tools of power.

"I assure myself," wrote Bacon to the King, "your
Majesty taketh not me for one of a busy nature ; for my
estate being free from all difficulties, and I having such a
large field for contemplation, as I have partly and shall
much more make manifest unto your Majesty and the
world, to occupy my thoughts, nothing could make me
active but love and affection." So Bacon described his
position with questionable accuracy—for his estate was not
"free from difficulties"—in the new time coming. He was
still kept out of the inner circle of the Council ; but from

H

the moment of Salisbury's death, he became a much more
important person.   He still sued for advancement, and
still met with disappointment; the "mean men" still rose
above him.   The lucrative place of Master of the Wards
was vacated by Salisbury's death.   Bacon was talked of
for it, and probably expected it, for he drew up new
rules for it, and a speech for the new master; but the
office and the speech went to Sir George Carey.   Soon after
Sir George Carey died.   Bacon then applied for it through
the new favourite, Rochester.   " He was so confident of
the place that he put most of his men into new cloaks;"
and the world of the day amused itself at his disappointment, when the place was given to another "mean man,"
Sir Walter Cope, of whom the gossips wrote that if the
"last two Treasurers could look out of their graves to see
those successors in that place, they would be out of countenance with themselves, and say to the world *quantum
mutatus.*"   But Bacon's hand and counsel appear more
and more in important matters—the improvement of
the revenue; the defence of extreme rights of the prerogative in the case against Whitelocke; the great question of calling a parliament, and of the true and "princely"
way of dealing with it.   His confidential advice to the
King about calling a parliament was marked by his keen
perception of the facts of the situation; it was marked
too by his confident reliance on skilful indirect methods
and trust in the look of things; it bears traces also of
his bitter feeling against Salisbury, whom he charges with
treacherously fomenting the opposition of the last Parliament.   There was no want of worldly wisdom in it;
certainly it was more adapted to James's ideas of state-
craft than the simpler plan of Sir Henry Nevill, that the

King should throw himself frankly on the loyalty and goodwill of Parliament. And thus he came to be on easy terms with James, who was quite capable of understanding Bacon's resource and nimbleness of wit. In the autumn of 1613, the Chief-Justiceship of the King's Bench became vacant. Bacon at once gave the King reasons for sending Coke from the Common Pleas—where he was a check on the prerogative — to the King's Bench, where he could do less harm; while Hobart went to the Common Pleas. The promotion was obvious; but the Common Pleas suited Coke better, and the place was more lucrative. Bacon's advice was followed. Coke, very reluctantly, knowing well who had given it, and why, "not only weeping himself but followed by the tears" of all the Court of Common Pleas, moved up to the higher post. The Attorney Hobart, succeeded; and Bacon at last became Attorney (October 27, 1613). In Chamberlain's gossip we have an indication, such as occurs only accidentally, of the view of outsiders : "There is a strong apprehension that little good is to be expected by this change, and that Bacon may prove a dangerous instrument."

CHAPTER V.

THUS, at last, at the age of fifty-two, Bacon had gained the place which Essex had tried to get for him at thirty-two. The time of waiting had been a weary one, and it is impossible not to see that it had been hurtful to Bacon. A strong and able man, very eager to have a field for his strength and ability, who is kept out of it, as he thinks unfairly, and is driven to an attitude of suppliant dependency in pressing his claim on great persons who amuse him with words, can hardly help suffering in the humiliating process. It does a man no good to learn to beg, and to have a long training in the art. And further, this long delay kept up the distraction of his mind between the noble work on which his soul was bent, and the necessities of that "civil" or professional and political life by which he had to maintain his estate. All the time that he was "canvassing" (it is his own word) for office, and giving up his time and thoughts to the work which it involved, the great *Instauration* had to wait his hours of leisure; and his exclamation, so often repeated, *Multum incola fuit anima mea*, bears witness to the longings that haunted him in his hours of legal drudgery, or in the service of his not very thankful employers. Not but that he found compensation in the interest of public questions, in the company of the great, in the excitement of state-craft and state employment, in the pomp and enjoyment of court life. He found too much compensation; it was one of his misfortunes. But his heart was always sound in its allegiance to knowledge; and if he had been fortunate enough to have risen earlier to the greatness which he aimed at as a vantage ground for his true work, or if he had had self-control to have dispensed with wealth and position—if he had escaped the long necessity of being a persistent and still baffled suitor—we might have had as a completed whole what we have now only in great fragments, and we should have been spared the blots which mar a career which ought to have been a noble one.

The first important matter that happened after Bacon's new appointment was the Essex divorce case, and the marriage of Lady Essex with the favourite whom Cecil's death had left at the height of power, and who from Lord Rochester was now made Earl of Somerset. With the divorce, the beginning of the scandals and tragedies of James's reign, Bacon had nothing to do. At the marriage which followed, Bacon presented as his offering a masque, performed by the members of Gray's Inn, of which he bore the charges, and which cost him the enormous sum of £2000. Whether it were to repay his obligations to the Howards, or in lieu of a "fee" to Rochester, who levied toll on all favours from the King, it can hardly be said, as has been suggested, to be a protest against the great abuse of the times, the sale of offices for money; the "very splendid trifle, the Masque of Flowers," was one form of the many extravagant

tributes paid but too willingly to high-handed worth-
lessness, of which the deeper and darker guilt was to
fill all faces with shame two years afterwards.

As Attorney, Bacon had to take a much more prominent part in affairs, legal, criminal, constitutional, ad-
ministrative, than he had yet been allowed to have. We
know that it was his great object to show how much
more active and useful an Attorney he could be than
either Coke or Hobart; and as far as unflagging energy
and high ability could make a good public servant, he
fully carried out his purpose. In Parliament, the "addled
Parliament" of 1614, in which he sat for the University of Cambridge, he did his best to reconcile what were
fast becoming irreconcilable, the claims and prerogatives
of an absolute king, irritable, suspicious, exacting, prodigal, with the ancient rights and liberties, growing
stronger in their demands by being denied, resisted, or
outwitted, of the popular element in the State. In the
trials, which are so large and disagreeable a part of the
history of these years, trials arising out of violent words
provoked by the violent acts of power, one of which,
Peacham's, became famous, because in the course of it
torture was resorted to—or trials which witnessed to the
corruption of the high society of the day, like the astound-
ing series of arraignments and condemnations following on
the discoveries relating to Overbury's murder, which had
happened just before the Somerset marriage—Bacon had
to make the best that he could for the cruel and often
unequal policy of the Court; and Bacon must take his
share in the responsibility for it. An effort on James's
part to stop duelling brought from Bacon a worthier piece
of service, in the shape of an earnest and elaborate argu-

ment against it, full of good sense and good feeling, but hopelessly in advance of the time. On the many questions which touched the prerogative, James found in his Attorney a ready and skilful advocate of his claims, who knew no limit to them, but in the consideration of what was safe and prudent to assert. He was a better and more statesmanlike counsellor, in his unceasing endeavours to reconcile James to the expediency of establishing solid and good relations with his Parliament, and in his advice as to the wise and hopeful ways of dealing with it. Bacon had no sympathy with popular wants and claims ; of popularity, of all that was called popular, he had the deepest suspicion and dislike ; the opinions and the judgment of average men he despised, as a thinker, a politician, and a courtier ; the "malignity of the people" he thought great. " I do not love," he says, "the word *people.*" But he had a high idea of what was worthy of a king, and was due to the public interests, and he saw the folly of the petty acts and haughty words, the use of which James could not resist. In his new office, he once more urged on, and urged in vain, his favourite project for revising, simplifying, and codifying the law. This was a project which would find little favour with Coke, and the crowd of lawyers who venerated him, men whom Bacon viewed with mingled contempt and apprehension both in the courts and in Parliament where they were numerous, and whom he more than once advised the King to bridle and keep " in awe." Bacon presented his scheme to the King in a Proposition, or, as we should call it, a Report. It is very able and interesting ; marked with his characteristic comprehensiveness and sense of practical needs, and with a confidence in his own know-

ledge of law which contrasts curiously with the current
opinion about it. He speaks with the utmost honour of
Coke's work ; but he is not afraid of a comparison with
him. "I do assure your Majesty," he says, "I am in
good hope, that when Sir Edward Coke's Reports and
my Rules and Decisions shall come to posterity, there
will be (whatever is now thought) question who was the
greater lawyer." But the project, though it was entertained and discussed in Parliament, came to nothing.
No one really cared about it except Bacon.

But in these years (1615 and 1616) two things happened of the utmost consequence to him. One was the
rise, more extravagant than anything that England had
seen for centuries, and in the end more fatal, of the new
favourite, who from plain George Villiers became the
all-powerful Duke of Buckingham. Bacon, like the rest
of the world, saw the necessity of bowing before him ;
and Bacon persuaded himself that Villiers was pre-emi-
nently endowed with all the gifts and virtues which a
man in his place would need. We have a series of his
letters to Villiers ; they are of course in the complimen-
tary vein which was expected ; but if their language is
only compliment, there is no language left for expressing
what a man wishes to be taken for truth. The other
matter was the humiliation, by Bacon's means and in his
presence, of his old rival Coke. In the dispute about
jurisdiction, always slumbering and lately awakened and
aggravated by Coke, between the Common Law Courts
and the Chancery, Coke had threatened the Chancery
with Præmunire. The King's jealousy took alarm, and
the Chief-Justice was called before the Council. There
a decree, based on Bacon's advice and probably drawn

up by him, peremptorily overruled the legal doctrine
maintained by the greatest and most self-confident judge
whom the English courts had seen. The. Chief-Justice
had to acquiesce in this reading of the law; and then, as
if such an affront were not enough, Coke was suspended
from his office, and, further, enjoined to review and amend
his published reports, where they were inconsistent with
the view of law which on Bacon's authority the Star
Chamber had adopted (June 1616). This he affected to
do; but the corrections were manifestly only colourable;
his explanations of his legal heresies against the prerogative, as these heresies were formulated by the Chancellor
and Bacon, and presented to him for recantation, were
judged insufficient; and in a decree, prefaced by reasons
drawn up by Bacon, in which, besides Coke's errors of
law, his "deceit, contempt, and slander of the Government," his "perpetual turbulent carriage," and his affectation of popularity, were noted,—he was removed from
his office (Nov. 1616). So, for the present, the old rivalry
had ended in a triumph for Bacon. Bacon, whom Coke
had so long headed in the race, whom he had sneered at
as a superficial pretender to law, and whose accomplish-
ments and enthusiasm for knowledge he utterly despised,
had not only defeated him, but driven him from his seat
with dishonour. When we remember what Coke was,
what he had thought of Bacon, and how he prized his
own unique reputation as a representative of English law,
the effects of such a disgrace on a man of his temper
cannot easily be exaggerated.

But for the present Bacon had broken through the
spell which had so long kept him back. He won a great
deal of the King's confidence, and the King was more

and more ready to make use of him, though by no means
equally willing to think that Bacon knew better than
himself.   Bacon's view of the law, and his resources of
argument and expression to make it good, could be depended upon in the keen struggle to secure and enlarge
the prerogative which was now beginning.   In this
prerogative both James and Bacon saw the safety of
the State and the only reasonable hope of good
government; but in Bacon's larger and more elevated
views of policy, of a policy worthy of a great king,
and a king of England, James was not likely to take
much interest.   The memorials which it was Bacon's
habit to present on public affairs were wasted on one
who had so little to learn from others,—so he thought
and so all assured him,—about the secrets of empire.
Still they were proofs of Bacon's ready mind ; and James,
even when he disagreed with Bacon's opinion and arguments, was too clever not to see their difference from the
work of other men.   Bacon rose in favour; and from
the first he was on the best of terms with Villiers.   He
professed to Villiers the most sincere devotion.   According to his custom he presented him with a letter of wise
advice on the duties and behaviour of a favourite.   He
at once began, and kept up with him to the end, a confidential correspondence on matters of public importance.
He made it clear that he depended upon Villiers for his
own personal prospects, and it had now become the most
natural thing that Bacon should look forward to succeeding the Lord Chancellor, Ellesmere, who was fast failing.
Bacon had already (Feb. 12, 16$\frac{1}{1}\frac{5}{6}$), in terms which seem
strange to us, but were less strange then, set forth in a
letter to the King the reasons why he should be Chan-

cellor; criticising justly enough, only that he was a party interested, the qualifications of other possible candidates, Coke, Hobart, and the Archbishop Abbott. Coke would be "an overruling nature in an overruling place," and "popular men were no sure mounters for your Majesty's saddle." Hobart was incompetent. As to Abbott, the Chancellor's place required "a whole man," and to have both jurisdiction, spiritual and temporal, "was fit only for a king." The promise that Bacon should have the place came to him three days afterwards through Villiers. He acknowledged it in a burst of gratitude (Feb. 15, $16\frac{15}{16}$). "I will now wholly rely on your excellent and happy self. . . . I am yours surer to you than my own life. For, as they speak of the Turquois stone in a ring, I will break into twenty pieces before you bear the least fall." They were unconsciously prophetic words. But Ellesmere lasted longer than was expected. It was not till a year after this promise that he resigned. On the 7th of March $16\frac{16}{17}$ Bacon received the seals. He expresses his obligations to Villiers, now Lord Buckingham, in the following letter :—

"MY DEAREST LORD—It is both in cares and kindness, that small ones float up to the tongue, and great ones sink down into the heart with silence. Therefore I could speak little to your Lordship to-day, neither had I fit time: but I must profess thus much, that in this day's work you are the truest and perfectest mirror and example of firm and generous friendship that ever was in court. And I shall count every day lost, wherein I shall not either study your well doing in thought, or do your name honour in speech, or perform you service in deed. Good my Lord, account and accept me, your most bounden and devoted friend and servant of all men living,

"March 7, 1616 (*i.e.* $\frac{1616}{1617}$).   FR. BACON, C.S."

He himself believed the appointment to be a popular

one. "I know I am come in," he writes to the King
soon after, "with as strong an envy of some particulars,
as with the love of the general." On the 7th of May
1617 he took his seat in Chancery with unusual pomp
and magnificence; and set forth, in an opening speech,
with all his dignity and force, the duties of his great
office, and his sense of their obligation. But there was
a curious hesitation in treating him as other men were
treated in like cases. He was only "Lord Keeper." It
was not till the following January (16$\frac{17}{18}$) that he received the office of Lord Chancellor. It was not till half
a year afterwards that he was made a Peer. Then he
became Baron Verulam (July 1618), and in January
16$\frac{20}{21}$ Viscount St. Alban's.

From this time Bacon must be thought of, first and
foremost, as a Judge in the great seat which he had so
earnestly sought. It was the place not merely of law,
which often tied the judge's hands painfully, but of
true justice, when law failed to give it. Bacon's ideas
of the duties of a judge were clear and strong, as he
showed in various admirable speeches and charges:
his duties as regards his own conduct and reputation;
his duties in keeping his subordinates free from the
taint of corruption. He was not ignorant of the subtle
and unacknowledged ways in which unlawful gains
may be covered by custom, and an abuse goes on because men will not choose to look at it. He entered
on his office with the full purpose of doing its work
better than it had ever been done. He saw where it
wanted reforming, and set himself at once to reform.
The accumulation and delay of suits had become grievous;
at once he threw his whole energy into the task of

wiping out the arrears which the bad health of his pre-
decessor, and the traditional sluggishness of the court,
had heaped up.   In exactly three months from his
appointment he was able to report that these arrears had
been cleared off.   "This day" (June 8, 1617), he writes
to Buckingham : "I have made even with the business
of the kingdom for common justice.   Not one cause
unheard.   The lawyers drawn dry of all the motions
they were to make.   Not one petition unheard.   And
this I think could not be said in our time before."

The performance was splendid, and there is no reason
to think that the work so rapidly done was not well
done.   We are assured that Bacon's decisions were
unquestioned and were not complained of.   At the same
time, before this allegation is accepted as conclusive
proof of the public satisfaction, it must be remembered
that the question of his administration of justice, which
was at last to assume such strange proportions, has never
been so thoroughly sifted as, to enable us to pronounce
upon it, it should be.   The natural tendency of Bacon's
mind would undoubtedly be to judge rightly and justly ;
but the negative argument of the silence at the time of
complainants, in days when it was so dangerous to
question authority, and when we have so little evidence
of what men said at their firesides, is not enough to show
that he never failed.

But the serious thing is that Bacon subjected himself
to two of the most dangerous influences which can act on
the mind of a judge—the influence of the most powerful
and most formidable man in England, and the influence
of presents, in money and other gifts.   From first to
last, he allowed Buckingham, whom no man, as Bacon

soon found, could displease except at his own peril, to
write letters to him on behalf of suitors whose causes
were before him; and he allowed suitors, not often
while the cause was pending, but sometimes even then,
to send him directly, or through his servants, large sums
of money. Both these things are explained. It would
have been characteristic of Bacon to be confident that
he could defy temptation : these habits were the fashion
of the time, and everybody took them for granted ;
Buckingham never asked his good offices beyond what
Bacon thought just and right, and asked them rather
for the sake of expedition, than to influence his judgment. And as to the money presents—every office was
underpaid ; this was the common way of acknowledging
pains and trouble ; it was analogous to a doctor's or a
lawyer's fee now. And there is no proof that either
influence ever led Bacon to do wrong. This has been said,
and said with some degree of force. But if it shows that
Bacon was not in this matter below his age, it shows that
he was not above it. No one knew better than Bacon
that there were no more certain dangers to honesty
and justice, than the interference and solicitation of the
great, and the old famous pest of bribes, of which all
histories and laws were full. And yet on the highest
seat of justice in the realm he, the great reformer of its
abuses, allowed them to make their customary haunt.
He did not mean to do wrong : his conscience was clear ;
he had not given thought to the mischief they must do,
sooner or later, to all concerned with the Court of
Chancery. With a magnificent carelessness he could
afford to run safely a course closely bordering on crime,
in which meaner men would sin and be ruined.

Before six months were over Bacon found on what
terms he must stand with Buckingham. By a strange
fatality, quite unintentionally, he became dragged into
the thick of the scandalous and grotesque dissensions of
the Coke family. The Court was away from London
in the North; and Coke had been trying, not without hope of success, to recover the King's favour.
Coke was a rich man, and Lady Compton, the mother
of the Villiers, thought that Coke's daughter would
be a good match for one of her younger sons. It
was really a great chance for Coke ; but he haggled
about the portion ; and the opportunity, which might
perhaps have led to his taking Bacon's place, passed.
But he found himself in trouble in other ways ; his
friends, especially Secretary Winwood, contrived to bring
the matter on again, and he consented to the Villiers's
terms. But his wife, the young lady's mother, Lady
Hatton, would not hear of it, and a furious quarrel followed. She carried off her daughter into the country.
Coke, with a warrant from Secretary Winwood, which
Bacon had refused to give him, pursued her : "with
his son, 'Fighting Clem,' and ten or eleven servants,
weaponed, in a violent manner, he repaired to the house
where she was remaining, and with a piece of timber or
form broke open the door and dragged her along to his
coach." Lady Hatton rushed off the same afternoon for
help to Bacon.

After an overturn by the way, "at last to my Lord Keeper's
they come, but could not have instant access to him for that his
people told them he was laid at rest, being not well. Then my
La. Hatton desired she might be in the next room where my Lord
lay, that she might be the first that [should] speak with him after
he was stirring. The door-keeper fulfilled her desire, and in the

meantime gave her a chair to rest herself in, and there left her
alone ; but not long after, she rose up and bounced against my
Lord Keeper's door, and waked him and affrighted him, that he
called his men to him ; and they opening the door, she thrust in
with them, and desired his Lp. to pardon her boldness, but she
was like a cow that had lost her calf, and so justified [herself] and
pacified my Lord's anger, and got his warrant and my Lo. Treasurer's warrant and others of the Council to fetch her daughter
from the father and bring them both to the Council."

It was a chance that the late Chief-Justice and his
wife, with their armed parties, did not meet on the road,
in which case "there were like to be strange tragedies."
At length the Council compelled both sides to keep
the peace, and the young lady was taken for the present
out of the hands of her raging parents.   Bacon had
assumed that the affair was the result of an intrigue
between Winwood and Coke, and that the Court would
take part against Coke, a man so deep in disgrace and
so outrageously violent.   Supposing that he had the ear
of Buckingham, he wrote earnestly persuading him to
put an end to the business : and in the meantime the
Council ordered Coke to be brought before the Star
Chamber "for riot and force," to "be heard and sentenced as justice shall appertain."   They had not the
slightest doubt that they were doing what would please
the King.   A few days after they met, and then they
learned the truth.

"Coke and his friends," writes Chamberlain, "complain of
hard measure from some of the greatest at that board, and that he
was too much trampled upon with ill language.   And our friend
[*i.e.* Winwood] passed out scot free for the warrant : which the
greatest [*word illegible*] there said was subject to a *præmunire ;*
and withal told the Lady Compton that they wished well to her
and her sons, and would be ready to serve the Earl of Buckingham
with all true affection, whereas others did it out of faction and

ambition :—which words glancing directly at our good friend
(Winwood), he was driven to make his apology ; and to show how
it was put upon him from time to time by the Queen and other
parties ; and, for conclusion, showed a letter of approbation of all
his courses from the King, making the whole table judge what
faction and ambition appeared in this carriage. *Ad quod non
fuit responsum.*"

None indeed, but blank faces, and thoughts of what
might come next. The Council, and Bacon foremost,
had made a desperate mistake. "It is evident," as Mr.
Spedding says, "that he had not divined Buckingham's
feelings on the subject." He was now to learn them.
To his utter amazement and alarm he found that the
King was strong for the match, and that the proceeding
of the Council was condemned at Court as gross mis-
conduct. In vain he protested that he was quite willing
to forward the match ; that in fact he had helped it.
Bacon's explanations and his warnings against Coke the
King "rejected with some disdain "; he justified Coke's
action ; he charged Bacon with disrespect and ingrati-
tude to Buckingham : he put aside his arguments and
apologies as worthless or insincere. Such reprimands
had not often been addressed, even to inferior servants.
Bacon's letters to Buckingham remained at first without
notice : when Buckingham answered, he did so with
scornful and menacing curtness. Meanwhile Bacon
heard from Yelverton how things were going at Court.

"Sir E. Coke," he wrote, "hath not forborne by any engine to
heave at both your Honour and myself, and he works the weightiest
instrument, the Earl of Buckingham, who, as I see, sets him as
close to him as his shirt, the Earl speaking in Sir Edward's phrase,
and as it were menacing in his spirit."

Buckingham, he went on to say, "did nobly and

I

plainly tell me he would not secretly bite, but whosoever
had had any interest, or tasted of the opposition to his
brother's marriage, he would as openly oppose them to
their faces, and they should discern what favour he had
by the power he would use." The Court, like a pack
of dogs, had set upon Bacon. "It is too common in
every man's mouth in Court, that your greatness shall
be abated, and as your tongue hath been as a razor unto
some, so shall theirs be to you." Buckingham said to
every one that Bacon had been forgetful of his kindness,
and unfaithful to him : "not forbearing in open speech
to tax you, as if it were an inveterate custom with you,
to be unfaithful unto him, as you were to the Earls of
Essex and Somerset."

All this while Bacon had been clearly in the right.
He had thrust himself into no business that did not
concern him. He had not, as Buckingham accuses
him of having done,—"overtroubled" himself with the
marriage. He had done his simple duty as a friend, as
a councillor, as a judge. He had been honestly zealous
for the Villiers's honour, and warned Buckingham of
things that were beyond question. He had curbed
Coke's scandalous violence, perhaps with no great regret, but with manifest reason. But for this, he was
now on the very edge of losing his office; it was clear
to him, as it is clear to us, that nothing could save him
but absolute submission. He accepted the condition.
How this submission was made and received, and with
what gratitude he found that he was forgiven, may be
seen in the two following letters. Buckingham thus
extends his grace to the Lord Keeper, and exhorts him
to better behaviour :—

"But his Majesty's direction in answer of your letter hath given me occasion to join hereunto a discovery unto you of mine inward thoughts, proceeding upon the discourse you had with me this day. For I do freely confess that your offer of submission unto me, and in writing (if so I would have it), battered so the unkindness that I had conceived in my heart for your behaviour towards me in my absence, as out of the sparks of my old affection toward you I went to sound his Majesty's intention how he means to behave himself towards you, specially in any public meeting ; where I found on the one part his Majesty so little satisfied with your late answer unto him, which he counted (for I protest I use his own terms) *confused and childish*, and his vigorous resolution on the other part so fixed, that he would put some public exemplary mark upon you, as I protest the sight of his deep-conceived indignation quenched my passion, making me upon the instant change from the person of a party into a peace-maker ; so as I was forced upon my knees to beg of his Majesty that he would put no public act of disgrace upon you, and, as I dare say, no other person would have been patiently heard in this suit by his Majesty but myself, so did I (though not without difficulty) obtain thus much :—that he would not so far disable you from the merit of your future service, as to put any particular mark of disgrace upon your person. Only thus far his Majesty protesteth, that upon the conscience of his office he cannot omit (though laying aside all passion) to give a kingly reprimand at his first sitting in council to so many of his councillors as were then here behind, and were actors in this business, for their ill behaviour in it. Some of the particular errors committed in this business he will name, but without accusing any particular persons by name.

"Thus your Lordship seeth the fruits of my natural inclination ; and I protest all this time past it was no small grief unto me to hear the mouth of so many upon this occasion open to load you with innumerable malicious and detracting speeches, as if no music were more pleasing to my ears than to rail of you : which made me rather regret the ill nature of mankind, that like dogs love to set upon him that they see once snatched at. And to conclude, my Lord, you have hereby a fair occasion so to make good hereafter your reputation by your sincere service to his Majesty, as also by your firm and constant kindness to your friends, as I may

(your Lordship's old friend) participate of the comfort and honour
that will thereby come to you.   Thus I rest at last
      "Your Lordship's faithful friend and servant,
                                                   "G. B."

   "MY EVER BEST LORD, now better than yourself—Your Lordship's pen, or rather pencil, hath pourtrayed towards me such
magnanimity and nobleness and true kindness, as methinketh I
see the image of some ancient virtue, and not anything of these
times.   It is the line of my life, and not the lines of my letter, that
must express my thankfulness : wherein if I fail, then God fail me,
and make me as miserable as I think myself at this time happy by
this reviver, through his Majesty's singular clemency, and your
incomparable love and favour.   God preserve you, prosper you,
and reward you for your kindness to
   "Your raised and infinitely obliged friend and servant,
"Sept. 22, 1617.   FR. BACON, C.S."

   Thus he had tried his strength with Buckingham.
He had found that this, "a little parent-like" manner of
advising him, and the doctrine that a true friend "ought
rather to go against his mind than his good," was not
what Buckingham expected from him.   And he never
ventured on it again.   It is not too much to say that a
man who could write as he now did to Buckingham, could
not trust himself, in any matter in which Buckingham
was interested.

   But the reconciliation was complete, and Bacon took
his place more and more as one of the chief persons in
the Government.   James claimed so much to have his
own way, and had so little scruple in putting aside, in his
superior wisdom, sometimes very curtly, Bacon's or any
other person's recommendations, that though his services
were great, and were not unrecognised, he never had the
power and influence in affairs to which his boundless
devotion to the Crown, his grasp of business, and his

willing industry, ought to have entitled him. He was still a servant, and made to feel it, though a servant in the "first form." It was James and Buckingham who determined the policy of the country, or settled the course to be taken in particular transactions; when this was settled, it was Bacon's business to carry it through successfully. In this he was like all the other servants of the Crown, and like them, he was satisfied with giving his advice, whether it were taken or not; but unlike many of them, he was zealous in executing with the utmost vigour and skill the instructions which were given him. Thus he was required to find the legal means for punishing Raleigh; and, as a matter of duty, he found them. He was required to tell the Government side of the story of Raleigh's crimes and punishment— which really was one side of the story, only not by any means the whole; and he told it, as he had told the Government story against Essex, with force, moderation, and good sense. Himself, he never would have made James's miserable blunders about Raleigh; but the blunders being made, it was his business to do his best to help the King out of them. When Suffolk, the Lord Treasurer, was disgraced and brought before the Star Chamber for corruption and embezzlement in his office, Bacon thought that he was doing no more than his duty in keeping Buckingham informed day by day how the trial was going on; how he had taken care that Suffolk's submission should not stop it—"for all would be but a play on the stage if justice went not on in the right course"—how he had taken care that the evidence went well—"I will not say I sometime holp it, as far as was fit for a judge"—how "a little to warm the

business " . . . " I spake a word, that he that did draw
or milk treasure from Ireland, did not, *emulgere,* milk
money, but blood." This, and other " little things " like
it, while he was sitting as a judge to try, if the word
may be used, a personal enemy of Buckingham, however
bad the case might be against Suffolk, sound strange
indeed to us ; and not less so when, in reporting the
sentence and the various opinions of the Council about
it, he, for once, praises Coke for the extravagance of his
severity :— " Sir Edward Coke did his part. I have not
heard him do better ; and began with a fine of £100,000,
but the judges first, and most of the rest, reduced it to
£30,000. I do not dislike that thing passed moderately ;
and all things considered, it is not amiss, and might
easily have been worse."

In all this, which would have been perfectly natural
from an Attorney-General of the time, Bacon saw but his
duty, even as a judge between the Crown and the subject.
It was what was expected of those whom the King chose
to employ, and whom Buckingham chose to favour. But a
worse and more cruel case, illustrating the system which
a man like Bacon could think reasonable and honourable, was the disgrace and punishment of Yelverton, the
Attorney-General, the man who had stood by Bacon,
and in his defence had faced Buckingham, knowing
well Buckingham's dislike of himself, when all the
Court turned against Bacon in his quarrel with Coke
and Lady Compton. Towards the end of the year 1620,
on the eve of a probable meeting of Parliament, there
was great questioning about what was to be done about
certain patents and monopolies—monopolies for making
gold and silk thread and for licensing inns and ale-

houses — which were in the hands of Buckingham's brothers and their agents. The monopolies were very unpopular; there was always doubt as to their legality; they were enforced oppressively and vexatiously by men like Michell and Mompesson, who acted for the Villiers; and the profits of them went, for the most part, not into the Exchequer, but into the pockets of the hangers-on of Buckingham. Bacon defended them both in law and policy, and his defence is thought by Mr. Gardiner to be not without grounds; but he saw the danger of obstinacy in maintaining what had become so hateful in the country, and strongly recommended that the more indefensible and unpopular patents should be spontaneously given up, the more so as they were of "no great fruit." But Buckingham's insolent perversity "refused to be convinced." The Council, when the question was before them, decided to maintain them. Bacon, who had rightly voted in the minority, thus explains his own vote to Buckingham:—"The King did wisely put it upon and consult, whether the patents were at this time to be removed by Act of Council before Parliament. *I opined (but yet somewhat like Ovid's mistress, that strove, but yet as one that would be overcome), that yes!*" But in the various disputes which had arisen about them, Yelverton had shown that he very much disliked the business of defending monopolies, and sending London citizens to jail for infringing them. He did it, but he did it grudgingly. It was a great offence in a man whom Buckingham had always disliked; and it is impossible to doubt that what followed was the consequence of his displeasure.

" In drawing up a new charter for the city of London," writes Mr.

Gardiner, Yelverton inserted clauses for which he was unable to produce a warrant. The worst that could be said was that he had, through inadvertence, misunderstood the verbal directions of the King. Although no imputation of corruption was brought against him, yet he was suspended from his office, and prosecuted in the Star Chamber. He was then sentenced to dismissal from his post, to a fine of £4000, and to imprisonment during the Royal pleasure."

In the management of this business Bacon had the chief part. Yelverton, on his suspension, at once submitted. The obnoxious clauses are not said to have been of serious importance ; but they were new clauses which the King had not sanctioned, and it would be a bad precedent to pass over such unauthorised additions even by an Attorney-General. "I mistook many things," said Yelverton afterwards in words which come back into our minds at a later period, "I was improvident in some things, and too credulous in all things." It might have seemed that dismissal, if not a severe reprimand, was punishment enough. But the submission was not enough, in Bacon's opinion, "for the King's honour." He dwelt on the greatness of the offence, and the necessity of making a severe example. According to his advice, Yelverton was prosecuted in the Star Chamber. It was not merely a mistake of judgment. "Herein," said Bacon, "I note the wisdom of the law of England, which termeth the highest contempt and excesses of authority, *Misprisions;* which (if you take the sound and derivation of the words) is but *mistaken ;* but if you take the use and acceptation of the word, it is high and heinous contempt and usurpation of authority ; whereof the reason I take to be and the name excellently imposed, for that main mistaking, it is ever joined with contempt ; for he that reveres will not easily mistake ; but he that

slights, and thinks more of the greatness of his place
than of the duty of his place, will soon commit misprisions." The day would come when this doctrine
would be pressed with ruinous effect against Bacon himself. But now he expounded with admirable clearness
the wrongness of carelessness about warrants and of
taking things for granted. He acquitted his former
colleague of "corruption of reward"; but "in truth that
makes the offence rather divers than less ;" for some
offences "are black, and others scarlet, some sordid,
some presumptuous." He pronounced his sentence—the
fine, the imprisonment; "for his place, I declare him
unfit for it." "And the next day," says Mr. Spedding,
"he reported to Buckingham the result of the proceeding," and takes no small credit for his own part in it.

It was thus that the Court used Bacon, and that
Bacon submitted to be used. He could have done, if he
had been listened to, much nobler service. He had from
the first seen, and urged as far as he could, the paramount
necessity of retrenchment in the King's profligate expenditure. Even Buckingham had come to feel the necessity
of it at last; and now that Bacon filled a seat at the
Council, and that the prosecution of Suffolk and an inquiry into the abuses of the Navy had forced on those in
power the urgency of economy, there was a chance of
something being done to bring order into the confusion
of the finances. Retrenchment began at the King's
kitchen and the tables of his servants; an effort was
made, not unsuccessfully, to extend it wider, under the
direction of Lionel Cranfield, a self-made man of business from the city; but with such a Court the task was
an impossible one. It was not Bacon's fault, though he

sadly mismanaged his own private affairs, that the King's
expenditure was not managed soberly and wisely. Nor
was it Bacon's fault, as far as advice went, that James
was always trying either to evade or to outwit a Parliament which he could not, like the Tudors, overawe.
Bacon's uniform counsel had been—Look on a Parliament as a certain necessity, but not only as a necessity ;
as also a unique and most precious means for uniting
the Crown with the nation, and proving to the world
outside how Englishmen love and honour their King,
and their King trusts his subjects.   Deal with it frankly
and nobly as becomes a king, not suspiciously like a
huckster in a bargain.   Do not be afraid of Parliament.
Be skilful in calling it ; but don't attempt to "pack" it.
Use all due adroitness and knowledge of human nature,
and necessary firmness and majesty, in managing it ;
keep unruly and mischievous people in their place ; but
do not be too anxious to meddle, "let nature work ;" and
above all, though of course you want money from it, do
not let that appear as the chief or real cause of calling
it.   Take the lead in legislation.   Be ready with some
interesting or imposing points of reform or policy, about
which you ask your Parliament to take counsel with you.
Take care to "frame and have ready some commonwealth
bills, that may add respect to the King's government,
and acknowledgment of his care ; not *wooing* bills to
make the King and his graces cheap ; but good matter
to set the Parliament on work, that an empty stomach
do not feed on humour."—So from the first had Bacon
always thought ; so he thought when he watched, as a
spectator, James's blunders with his first Parliament of
1604 ; so had he earnestly counselled James, when ad-

mitted to his confidence, as to the Parliaments of 1614
and 1615; so again, but in vain, as Chancellor, he
advised him to meet the Parliament of 1620. It was
wise, and from his point of view, honest advice, though
there runs all through it too much reliance on appearances which were not all that they seemed; there was
too much thought of throwing dust in the eyes of
troublesome and inconvenient people. But whatever
motives there might have been behind, it would have
been well if James had learned from Bacon how to deal
with Englishmen. But he could not. "I wonder," said
James one day to Gondomar, "that my ancestors should
ever have permitted such an institution as the House of
Commons to have come into existence. I am a stranger,
and found it here when I arrived, so that I am obliged
to put up with what I cannot get rid of." James was
the only one of our many foreign kings who, to the last,
struggled to avoid submitting himself to the conditions
of an English throne.

CHAPTER VI.

WHEN Parliament met on January 30, $16\frac{20}{21}$, and Bacon,
as Lord Chancellor, set forth in his ceremonial speeches,
to the King and to the Speaker, the glories and blessings
of James's reign, no man in England had more reason
to think himself fortunate. He had reached the age of
sixty, and had gained the object of his ambition. More
than that, he was conscious that in his great office he
was finding full play for his powers, and his high public
purposes. He had won greatly on the confidence of the
King. He had just received a fresh mark of honour
from him; a few days before he had been raised a step
in the peerage, and he was now Viscount St. Alban's.
With Buckingham he seemed to be on terms of the
most affectionate familiarity, exchanging opinions freely
with him on every subject. And Parliament met in
good humour. They voted money at once. One of the
matters which interested Bacon most—the revision of
the Statute Book—they took up as one of their first
measures, and appointed a Select Committee to report
upon it. And what, amid the apparent felicity of the
time, was of even greater personal happiness to Bacon,
the first step of the "Great Instauration" had been

taken. During the previous autumn, Oct. 12, 1620, the
Novum Organum, the first instalment of his vast design,
was published, the result of the work of thirty years;
and copies were distributed to great people, among
others to Coke. He apprehended no evil; he had nothing to fear, and much to hope from the times.

His sudden and unexpected fall, so astonishing and
so irreparably complete, is one of the strangest events of
that still imperfectly comprehended time. There had
been, and were still to be, plenty of instances of the
downfall of power, as ruinous and even more tragic;
though scarcely any one more pathetic in its surprise
and its shame. But it is hard to find one of which
so little warning was given, and the causes of which are
at once in part so clear, and in part so obscure and unintelligible. Such disasters had to be reckoned upon as
possible chances by any one who ventured into public
life. Montaigne advises that the discipline of pain
should be part of every boy's education, for the reason
that every one in his day might be called upon to under-
go the torture. And so every public man, in the England
of the Tudors and Stuarts, entered on his career with
the perfectly familiar expectation of possibly closing it,
it might be in an honourable and ceremonious fashion,
in the Tower and on the scaffold; just as he had to look
forward to the possibility of closing it by smallpox or
the plague. So that when disaster came, though it
might be unexpected as death is unexpected, it was a
turn of things which ought not to take a man by surprise.
But some premonitory signs usually gave warning.
There was nothing to warn Bacon that the work which
he believed he was doing so well would be interrupted.

We look in vain for any threatenings of the storm.
What the men of his time thought and felt about Bacon
it is not easy to ascertain. Appearances are faint and
contradictory ; he himself, though scornful of judges who
sought to be "popular," believed that he "came in with
the favour of the general ;" that he "had a little popular
reputation, which followeth me, whether I will or no."
No one, for years, had discharged the duties of his office
with greater efficiency.   Scarcely a trace remains of any
suspicion, previous to the attack upon him, of the justice
of his decisions ; no instance was alleged that, in fact, im-
pure motives had controlled the strength and lucidity of
an intellect which loved to be true and right for the mere
pleasure of being so.   Nor was there anything in Bacon's
political position to make him specially obnoxious above
all others of the King's Council. He maintained the
highest doctrines of prerogative ; but they were current
doctrines, both at the Council board and on the bench ;
and they were not discredited nor extinguished by his
fall.   To be on good terms with James and Buckingham
meant a degree of subservience which shocks us now ;
but it did not shock people then, and he did not differ
from his fellows in regarding it as part of his duty as a
public servant of the Crown.   No doubt he had enemies
—some with old grudges like Southampton, who had
been condemned with Essex; some like Suffolk, smarting
under recent reprimands and the biting edge of Bacon's
tongue ; some, like Coke, hating him from constitutional
antipathies and the strong antagonism of professional
doctrines, for a long ourse of rivalry, and for mortifying
defeats.   But there is no appearance of preconcerted
efforts among them to bring about his overthrow.   He

did not, at the time, seem to be identified with anything
dangerous or odious. There was no doubt a good deal
of dissatisfaction with Chancery—among the common
lawyers, because it interfered with their business; in
the public, partly from the traditions of its slowness,
partly from its expensiveness, partly because being intended for special redress of legal hardship it was sure
to disappoint one party to a suit. But Bacon thought
that he had reformed Chancery. He had also done a
great deal to bring some kind of order, or at least hopefulness of order, into the King's desperate finances.
And he had never set himself against Parliament. On
the contrary, he had always been forward to declare that
the King could not do without Parliament, and that
Parliament only needed to be dealt with generously, and
as " became a King," to be not a danger and hindrance to
the Crown, but its most sincere and trustworthy support.

What was then to portend danger to Bacon when
the Parliament of 16$\frac{20}{21}$ met ? The House of Commons
at its meeting was thoroughly loyal and respectful ; it
meant to be *benedictum et pacificum parliamentum.*
Every one knew that there would be "grievances"
which would not be welcome to the Court; but they
did not seem likely to touch him. Every one knew that
there would be questions raised about unpopular patents
and oppressive monopolies, and about their legality ;
and it was pretty well agreed upon at Court, that they
should be given up as soon as complained of. But
Bacon was not implicated more than the Crown lawyers
before him, in what all the Crown lawyers had always
defended. There was dissatisfaction about the King's
extravagance and wastefulness, about his indecision in

the cause of the Elector Palatine, about his supposed
intrigues with Papistical and tyrannical Spain; but Bacon
had nothing to do with all this except, as far as he
could, to give wise counsel and warning. The person
who made the King despised and hated was the splendid
and insolent favourite, Buckingham. It might have
been thought that the one thing to be set against much
that was wrong in the State was the just and enlightened
and speedy administration of equity in the Chancery.

When Parliament met, though nothing seemed to
threaten mischief, it met with a sturdy purpose of bringing to account certain delinquents whose arrogance and
vexations of the subjects had provoked the country, and
who were supposed to shelter themselves under the
countenance of Buckingham.   Michell and Mompesson
were rascals whose misdemeanours might well try the
patience of a less spirited body than an English House of
Commons. Buckingham could not protect them, and
hardly tried to do so.   But just as one electric current
" induces " another by neighbourhood, so all this deep indignation against Buckingham's creatures created a fierce
temper of suspicion about corruption all through the public
service. Two Committees were early appointed by the
House of Commons; one a Committee on Grievances,
such as the monopolies; the other, a Committee to in-
quire into abuses in the Courts of Justice and receive
petitions about them.   In the course of the proceedings,
the question arose in the House as to the authorities or
"Referees" who had certified to the legality of the
Crown patents or grants which had been so grossly
abused ; and among these " referees " were the Lord
Chancellor and other high officers, both legal and political.

It was the little cloud. But lookers-on like Chamberlain did not think much of it.   " The referees," he wrote
on Feb. 29, " who certified the legality of the patents
are glanced at, but they are chiefly above the reach of
the House ; they attempt so much that they will accomplish little."   Coke, who was now the chief leader in
Parliament, began to talk ominously of precedents, and
to lay down rules about the power of the House to
punish—rules which were afterwards found to have no
authority for them.   Cranfield, the representative of
severe economy, insisted that the honour of the King
required that the referees, whoever they were, should be
called to account.   The gathering clouds shifted a little,
when the sense of the House seemed to incline to giving
up all retrospective action, and to a limitation for the
future by statute of the questionable prerogative — a
limitation which was in fact attempted by a bill thrown
out by the Lords.   But they gathered again when
the Commons determined to bring the whole matter
before the House of Lords.   The King wrote to warn
Bacon of what was coming.   The proposed conference
was staved off by management for a day or two ; but
it could not be averted : and the Lords showed their
eagerness for it.   And two things by this time, the
beginning of March, seemed now to have become clear,
first, that under the general attack on the referees was
intended a blow against Bacon ; next, that the person
whom he had most reason to fear was Sir Edward
Coke.

The storm was growing ; but Bacon was still un-
alarmed, though Buckingham had been frightened into
throwing the blame on the referees.

K

"I do hear," he writes to Buckingham (dating his letter on March
7, 'the day I received the seal'), "from divers of judgement, that
to-morrow's conference is like to pass in a calm, as to the referees.
Sir Lionel Cranfield, who hath been formerly the trumpet, said
yesterday, that he did now incline unto Sir John Walter's opinion
and motion not to have the referees meddled with, otherwise than
to discount it from the King; and so not to look back, but to the
future.   And I do hear almost all men of judgement in the
house wish now that way.   I woo nobody; I do but listen, and I
have doubt only of Sir Edward Coke, who I wish had some round
caveat given him from the King: for your Lordship hath no great
power with him.   But a word from the King mates him."

But Coke's opportunity had come.   The House of
Commons was disposed for gentler measures.   But he
was able to make it listen to his harsher counsels, and
from this time his hand appears in all that was done.
The first conference was a tame and dull one.   The
spokesmen had been slack in their disagreeable and
perhaps dangerous duty.   But Coke and his friends
took them sharply to task.   "The heart and tongue
of Sir Edward Coke are true relations," said one of his
fervent supporters; "but his pains hath not reaped that
harvest of praise that he hath deserved.   For the
Referees, they are as transcendent delinquents as any
other, and sure their souls made a wilful elopement
from their bodies when they made these certificates."
A second conference was held with the Lords, and this
time the charge was driven home.   The referees were
named, the Chancellor at the head of them.   When
Bacon rose to explain and justify his acts, he was sharply
stopped, and reminded that he was transgressing the
orders of the House in speaking till the Committees
were named to examine the matter.   What was even
more important, the King had come to the House of

Lords (March 10), and frightened, perhaps, about his
subsidies, told them "that he was not guilty of those
grievances which are now discovered, but that he
grounded his judgement upon others who have misled
him." The referees would be attacked, people thought,
if the Lower House had courage.

All this was serious. As things were drifting, it
seemed as if Bacon might have to fight the legal question
of the prerogative in the form of a criminal charge, and
be called upon to answer the accusation of being the
minister of a crown which legal language pronounced
absolute, and of a King who interpreted legal language
to the letter; and further, to meet his accusers after the
King himself had disavowed what his servant had done.
What passed between Bacon and the King is confused
and uncertain; but after his speech the King could
scarcely have thought of interfering with the inquiry.
The proceedings went on; Committees were named for
the several points of inquiry; and Bacon took part in
these arrangements. It was a dangerous position to have
to defend himself against an angry House of Commons,
led and animated by Coke and Cranfield. But though
the storm had rapidly thickened, the charges against
the referees were not against him alone. His mistake
in law, if it was a mistake, was shared by some of the
first lawyers and first councillors in England. There
was a battle before him, but not a hopeless one. "*Modicæ
fidei, quare dubitasti,*" he writes about this time to an
anxious friend.

But in truth the thickening storm had been gathering
over his head alone. It was against him that the whole
attack was directed; as soon as it took a different

shape, the complaints against the other referees, such
as the Chief-Justice, who was now Lord Treasurer,
though some attempt was made to press them, were
quietly dropped.   What was the secret history of these
weeks we do not know.   But the result of Bacon's ruin
was that Buckingham was saved.   "As they speak of
the Turquois stone in a ring," Bacon had said to Buckingham, when he was made Chancellor, "I will break
into twenty pieces, before you have the least fall."
Without knowing what he pledged himself to, he was
taken at his word.

At length the lightning fell.   During the early part
of March, while these dangerous questions were mooted
about the referees, a Committee, appointed early in the
session, had also been sitting on abuses in courts of
justice, and as part of their business, an inquiry had
been going on into the ways of the subordinate officers
of the Court of Chancery.   Bacon had early (Feb. 17)
sent a message to the Committee courting full inquiry,
"willingly consenting that any man might speak
anything of his Court."   On the 12th of March
the chairman, Sir R. Philips, reported that he had
in his hands "divers petitions, many frivolous and
clamorous, many of weight and consequence."   Cranfield, who presided over the Court of Wards, had
quarrelled fiercely with the Chancery, where he said
there was "neither Law, Equity, or Conscience," and
pressed the inquiry, partly, it may be, to screen his own
Court, which was found fault with by the lawyers.
Some scandalous abuses were brought to light in the
Chancery.   They showed that "Bacon was at fault in
the art of government," and did not know how to keep

his servants in order. One of them, John Churchill, an
infamous forger of Chancery orders, finding things going
hard with him, and "resolved," it is said, "not to sink
alone," offered his confessions of all that was going on
wrong in the Court. But on the 15th of March things
took another turn. It was no longer a matter of doubtful constitutional law; no longer a question of slack
discipline over his officers. To the astonishment, if not
of the men of his own day, at least to the unexhausted
astonishment of times following, a charge was suddenly
reported from the Committee to the Commons against
the Lord Chancellor, not of straining the prerogative, or
of conniving at his servants' misdoings, but of being
himself a corrupt and venal judge. Two suitors charged
him with receiving bribes. Bacon was beginning to feel
worried and anxious, and he wrote thus to Buckingham.
At length he had begun to see the meaning of all these
inquiries, and to what they were driving.

"MY VERY GOOD LORD—Your Lordship spake of Purgatory.
I am now in it, but my mind is in a calm; for my fortune is not
my felicity. I know I have clean hands and a clean heart ; and I
hope a clean house for friends or servants. But Job himself, or
whosoever was the justest judge, by such hunting for matters
against him as hath been used against me, may for a time seem
foul, specially in a time when greatness is the mark, and accusation
is the game. And if this be to be a Chancellor, I think if the
great seal lay upon Hounslow Heath, nobody would take it up. But
the King and your Lordship will, I hope, put an end to these miseries
one way or other. And in troth that which I fear most is lest
continual attendance and business, together with these cares, and
want of time to do my weak body right this spring by diet and
physic, will cast me down ; and then it will be thought feigning
or fainting. But I hope in God I shall hold out. God prosper
you."

The first charges attracted others, which were made
formal matters of complaint by the House of Commons.
John Churchill, to save himself, was busy setting down
cases of misdoing; and probably suitors of themselves
became ready to volunteer evidence. But of this Bacon
as yet knew nothing. He was at this time only aware
that there were persons who were "hunting out complaints against him," that the attack was changed from
his law to his private character; he had found an unfavourable feeling in the House of Lords : and he knew
well enough what it was to have powerful enemies in
those days when a sentence was often settled before a
trial. To any one, such a state of things was as formidable as the first serious symptoms of a fever. He was
uneasy, as a man might well be, on whom the House of
Commons had fixed its eye, and to whom the House of
Lords had shown itself unfriendly. But he was as yet
conscious of nothing fatal to his defence, and he knew
that if false accusations could be lightly made they could
also be exposed.

A few days after the first mention of corruption
the Commons laid their complaints of him before the
House of Lords, and on the same day (March 19), Bacon,
finding himself too ill to go to the House, wrote to the
Peers by Buckingham, requesting them that as some
"complaints of base bribery" had come before them,
they would give him a fair opportunity of defending
himself, and of cross-examining witnesses; especially
begging, that considering the number of decrees which
he had to make in a year, more than two thousand, and
" the courses which had been taken in hunting out complaints against him," they would not let their opinion of

him be affected by the mere number of charges that might be made. Their short verbal answer, moved by Southampton (March 20), that they meant to proceed by right rule of justice, and would be glad if he cleared his honour, was not encouraging. And now that the Commons had brought the matter before them, the Lords took it entirely into their own hands, appointing three Committees, and examining the witnesses themselves. New witnesses came forward every day with fresh cases of gifts and presents, "bribes," received by the Lord Chancellor. When Parliament rose for the Easter vacation (March 27—April 17), the Committees continued sitting. A good deal probably passed of which no record remains. When the Commons met again (April 17) Coke was full of gibes about *Instauratio Magna;* the true *Instauratio* was to restore laws; and two days after an Act was brought in for review and reversal of decrees in Courts of Equity. It was now clear that the case against Bacon had assumed formidable dimensions, and also a very strange, and almost monstrous shape. For the Lords, who were to be the judges, had by their Committees taken the matter out of the hands of the Commons, the original accusers, and had become themselves the prosecutors, collecting and arranging evidence, accepting or rejecting depositions, and doing all that counsel or the committing magistrate would do preliminary to a trial. There appears to have been no cross-examining of witnesses on Bacon's behalf, or hearing witnesses for him; not unnaturally at this stage of business, when the prosecutors were engaged in making out their own case; but considering that the future judges had of their own accord turned themselves into the prosecutors, the unfairness was great. At the same time it does not appear that Bacon did anything to watch how things went in the Committees, which had his friends in them as well as his enemies, and are said to have been open courts. Towards the end of March Chamberlain wrote to Carleton that "the Houses were working hard at cleansing out the Augæan stable of monopolies, and also extortions in Courts of Justice. The petitions against the Lord Chancellor were too numerous to be got through: his chief friends and brokers of bargains, Sir George Hastings, and Sir Richard Young, and others attacked, are obliged to accuse him in their own defence, though very reluctantly. His ordinary bribes were £300, £400, and even £1000. . . . The Lords admit no evidence except on oath. One Churchill, who was dismissed from the Chancery Court for extortion, is the chief cause of the Chancellor's ruin." [1] Bacon was greatly alarmed. He wrote to Buckingham, who was "his anchor in these floods." He wrote to the King; he was at a loss to account for the "tempest that had come on him": he could not understand what he had done to offend the country or Parliament: he had never "taken rewards to pervert justice, however he might be frail, and partake of the abuse of the time."

"Time hath been when I have brought unto you *gemitum columbæ* from others. Now I bring it from myself. I fly unto your Majesty with the wings of a dove, which once within these seven days I thought would have carried me a higher flight.

"When I enter into myself, I find not the materials of such a tempest as is comen upon me. I have been (as your Majesty knoweth best), never author of any immoderate counsel, but always desired to have things carried *suavibus modis*. I have been no

---

[1] *Calendar of State Papers* (domestic), March 24, 1621.

avaricious oppressor of the people.   I have been no haughty or
intolerable or hateful man, in my conversation or carriage.   I have
inherited no hatred from my father, but am a good patriot born.
Whence should this be?   For these are the things that use to raise
dislikes abroad."

And he ended by entreating the King to help him :

"That which I thirst after, as the hart after the streams, is that
I may know by my matchless friend [Buckingham] that presenteth
to you this letter, your Majesty's heart (which is an *abyssus* of
goodness, as I am an *abyssus* of misery) towards me.   I have been
ever your man, and counted myself but an usufructuary of myself,
the property being yours : and now making myself an oblation to
do with me as may best conduce to the honour of your justice, the
honour of your mercy, and the use of your service, resting as
        "Clay in your Majesty's gracious hands,

                                "FR. ST. ALBAN, Canc.
    "March 25, 1621."

To the world he kept up an undismayed countenance :
he went down to Gorhambury, attended by troops of
friends.   "This man," said Prince Charles, when he met
his company, "scorns to go out like a snuff."   But at
Gorhambury he made his will, leaving "his name to the
next ages, and to foreign nations ; " and he wrote a prayer,
which is a touching evidence of his state of mind :—

"Most gracious Lord God, my merciful Father, from my youth
up, my Creator, my Redeemer, my Comforter.   Thou (O Lord)
soundest and searchest the depths and secrets of all hearts ; thou
knowledgest the upright of heart, thou judgest the hypocrite, thou
ponderest men's thoughts and doings as in a balance, thou measurest
their intentions as with a line, vanity and crooked ways cannot be
hid from thee.

"Remember (O Lord) how thy servant hath walked before
thee ; remember what I have first sought, and what hath been
principal in mine intentions.   I have loved thy assemblies, I have
mourned for the divisions of thy Church, I have delighted in the

brightness of thy sanctuary. This vine which thy right hand hath planted in this nation, I have ever prayed unto thee that it might have the first and the latter rain ; and that it might stretch her branches to the seas and to the floods. The state and bread of the poor and oppressed have been precious in my eyes : I have hated all cruelty and hardness of heart ; I have (though in a despised weed) procured the good of all men. If any have been mine enemies, I thought not of them ; neither hath the sun almost set upon my displeasure ; but I have been as a dove, free from super-fluity of maliciousness. Thy creatures have been my books, but thy Scriptures much more. I have sought thee in the courts, fields, and gardens, but I have found thee in thy temples.

"Thousand have been my sins, and ten thousand my trans-gressions ; but thy sanctifications have remained with me, and my heart, through thy grace, hath been an unquenched coal upon thy altar. O Lord, my strength, I have since my youth met with thee in all my ways, by thy fatherly compassions, by thy comfort-able chastisements, and by thy most visible providence. As thy favours have increased upon me, so have thy corrections ; so as thou hast been alway near me, O Lord ; and ever as my worldly blessings were exalted, so secret darts from thee have pierced me ; and when I have ascended before men, I have descended in humilia-tion before thee.

"And now when I thought most of peace and honour, thy hand is heavy upon me, and hath humbled me, according to thy former loving-kindness, keeping me still in thy fatherly school, not as a bastard, but as a child. Just are thy judgements upon me for my sins, which are more in number than the sands of the sea, but have no proportion to thy mercies ; for what are the sands of the sea, to the sea, earth, heavens ? and all these are nothing to thy mercies.

" Besides my innumerable sins, I confess before thee that I am debtor to thee for the gracious talent of thy gifts and graces, which I have misspent in things for which I was least fit ; so as I may truly say, my soul hath been a stranger in the course of my pilgrimage. Be merciful unto me (O Lord) for my Saviour's sake, and receive me into thy bosom, or guide me in thy ways."

Bacon up to this time, strangely, if the Committees

were " open Courts," was entirely ignorant of the
particulars of the charge which was accumulating
against him.   He had an interview with the King,
which was duly reported to the House, and he placed
his case before James, distinguishing between the
" three cases of bribery supposed in a judge—a corrupt
bargain ; carelessness in receiving a gift while the cause
is going on ; and, what is innocent, receiving a gift after
it is ended." And he meant in such words as these to
place himself at the King's disposal, and ask his direction :—

> " For my fortune, *summa summarum* with me is, that I may
> not be made altogether unprofitable to do your Majesty service or
> honour. If your Majesty continue me as I am, I hope I shall be a
> new man, and shall reform things out of feeling, more than another
> can do out of example. If I cast part of my burden, I shall be
> more strong and *delivré* to bear the rest. And, to tell your
> Majesty what my thoughts run upon, I think of writing a story
> of England, and of recompiling of your laws into a better digest."

The King referred him to the House ; and the House
now (April 19) prepared to gather up into " one brief "
the charges against the Lord Chancellor, still, however,
continuing open to receive fresh complaints.

Meanwhile the chase after abuses of all kinds was
growing hotter in the Commons—abuses in patents and
monopolies, which revived the complaints against referees,
among whom Bacon was frequently named, and abuses
in the Courts of Justice.   The attack passed by and
spared the Common Law Courts, as was noticed in the
course of the debates ; it spared Cranfield's Court, the
Court of Wards.   But it fell heavily on the Chancery
and the Ecclesiastical Courts.   " I have neither power

nor will to defend Chancery," said Sir John Bennett, the
judge of the Prerogative Court ; but a few weeks after
his turn came, and a series of as ugly charges as could
well be preferred against a judge, charges of extortion
as well as bribery, were reported to the House by its
Committee. There can be no doubt of the grossness of
many of these abuses, and the zeal against them was
honest, though it would have shown more courage if it had
flown at higher game ; but the daily discussion of them
helped to keep alive and inflame the general feeling
against so great a "delinquent" as the Lord Chancellor
was supposed to be. And, indeed, two of the worst
charges against him were made before the Commons.
One was a statement made in the House by Sir George
Hastings, a member of the House, who had been the
channel of Awbry's gift, that when he had told Bacon
that if questioned he must admit it, Bacon's answer
was : "George, if you do so, I must deny it upon my
honour—upon my oath." The other was that he had
given an opinion in favour of some claim of the Masters
in Chancery for which he received £1200, and with
which he said that all the judges agreed—an assertion
which all the judges denied. Of these charges there is
no contradiction.[1]

Bacon made one more appeal to the King (April 21).
He hoped that, by resigning the seal, he might be spared
the sentence :—

"But now if not *per omnipotentiam* (as the divines speak), but
per potestatem suaviter disponentem, your Majesty will graciously
save me from a sentence with the good liking of the House, and
that cup may pass from me ; it is the utmost of my desires.

[1] *Commons' Journals,* March 17, April 27 ; iii. 560, 594-6.

" This I move with the more belief, because I assure myself that
if it be reformation that is sought, the very taking away the seal,
upon my general submission, will be as much in example for these
four hundred years, as any furder severity."

At length, informally, but for the first time distinctly,
the full nature of the accusation, with its overwhelming
list of cases, came to Bacon's knowledge (April 20 or
21). From the single charge, made in the middle of
March, it had swelled in force and volume like a
rising mountain torrent. That all these charges should
have sprung out of the ground from their long conceal-
ment is strange enough. How is it that nothing was
heard of them when the things happened? And what is
equally strange is that these charges were substantially
true and undeniable; that this great Lord Chancellor, so
admirable in his despatch of business, hitherto so little
complained of for wrong or unfair decisions, had been in
the habit of receiving large sums of money from suitors,
in some cases certainly while the suit was pending. And
further, while receiving them, while perfectly aware of
the evil of receiving gifts on the seat of judgment, while
emphatically warning inferior judges against yielding to
the temptation, he seems really to have continued unconscious of any wrong-doing while gift after gift was
offered and accepted. But nothing is so strange as the
way in which Bacon met the charges. Tremendous as
the accusation was, he made not the slightest fight about
it. Up to this time he had held himself innocent.
Now, overwhelmed and stunned, he made no attempt at
defence; he threw up the game without a struggle, and
volunteered an absolute and unreserved confession of
his guilt—that is to say, he declined to stand his trial.

Only, he made an earnest application to the House of
Lords, in proceeding to sentence, to be content with a
general admission of guilt, and to spare him the humiliation of confessing the separate facts of alleged "bribery"
which were contained in the twenty-eight articles of
his accusation. This submission, "grounded only on
rumour," for the Articles of charge had not yet been
communicated to him by the accusers, took the House
by surprise. "No Lord spoke to it, after it had been
read, for a long time." But they did not mean that he
should escape with this. The House treated the suggestion with impatient scorn (April 24). "It is too
late," said Lord Saye. "No word of confession of any
corruption in the Lord Chancellor's submission," said
Southampton; "it stands with the justice and honour
of this House not to proceed without the parties' particular confession, or to have the parties to hear the
charge, and we to hear the parties answer." The
demand of the Lords was strictly just, but cruel; the
Articles were now sent to him; he had been charged
with definite offences; he must answer yes or no, confess them or defend himself. A further question arose
whether he should not be sent for to appear at the bar.
He still held the seals. "Shall the Great Seal come to
the bar?" asked Lord Pembroke. It was agreed that he
was to be asked whether he would acknowledge the
particulars. His answer was "that he will make no
manner of defence to the charge, but meaneth to
acknowledge corruption, and to make a particular confession to every point, and after that a humble submission. But he humbly craves liberty that, when the
charge is more full than he finds the truth of the fact he

may make a declaration of the truth in such particulars,
the charge being brief and containing not all the circumstances." And such a confession he made. "My
Lords," he said, to those who were sent to ask whether
he would stand to it, "it is my act, my hand, my heart.
I beseech your Lordships be merciful to a broken
reed." This was of course followed by a request to the
King from the House to "sequester" the Great Seal. A
commission was sent to receive it (May 1). "The worse,
the better," he answered to the wish "that it had been
better with him." "By the King's great favour I
received the Great Seal; by my own great fault I have
lost it." They intended him now to come to the bar to
receive his sentence. But he was too ill to leave his bed.
They did not push this point farther, but proceeded to
settle the sentence (May 3). He had asked for mercy,
but he did not get it. There were men who talked of
every extremity short of death. Coke, indeed, in the
Commons, from his store of precedents, had cited cases
where judges had been hanged for bribery. But the Lords
would not hear of this. "His offences foul," said Lord
Arundel; "his confession pitiful. Life not to be touched."
But Southampton, whom twenty years before he had
helped to involve in Essex's ruin, urged that he should
be degraded from the peerage; and asked whether, at
any rate, "he whom this House thinks unfit to be a
constable shall come to the Parliament." He was fined
£40,000. He was to be imprisoned in the Tower during
the King's pleasure. He was to be incapable of any
office, place, or employment in the State or Commonwealth. He was never to sit in Parliament or come
within the verge of the Court. This was agreed to,

Buckingham only dissenting. "The Lord Chancellor is
so sick," he said, "that he cannot live long."

What is the history of this tremendous catastrophe
by which, in less than two months, Bacon was cast down
from the height of fortune to become a byword of shame?
He had enemies, who certainly were glad, but there is
no appearance that it was the result of any plot or combination against him. He was involved, accidentally, it
may almost be said, in the burst of anger excited by the
intolerable dealings of others. The indignation provoked
by Michell and Mompesson and their associates at that
particular moment found Bacon in its path, doing, as it
seemed, in his great seat of justice, even worse than they;
and when he threw up all attempt at defence, and his
judges had his hand to an unreserved confession of corruption, both generally, and in the long list of cases alleged
against him, it is not wonderful that they came to the
conclusion, as the rest of the world did, that he was as
bad as the accusation painted him—a dishonest and corrupt judge. Yet it is strange that they should not have
observed that not a single charge of a definitely unjust
decision was brought, at any rate was proved, against
him. He had taken money, they argued, and therefore
he must be corrupt; but if he had taken money to pervert judgment, some instance of the iniquity would certainly have been brought forward and proved. There
is no such instance to be found; though, of course, there
were plenty of dissatisfied suitors; of course the men
who had paid their money and lost their cause were
furious. But in vain do we look for any case of proved
injustice. The utmost that can be said is that in some
cases he showed favour in pushing forward and expedit-

ing suits. So that the real charge against Bacon assumes,
to us who have not to deal practically with dangerous
abuses, but to judge conduct and character, a different
complexion. Instead of being the wickedness of per-
verting justice and selling his judgments for bribes, it
takes the shape of allowing and sharing in a dishonour-
able and mischievous system of payment for service,
which could not fail to bring with it temptation and
discredit, and in which fair reward could not be distinguished from unlawful gain.   Such a system it was high
time to stop; and in this rough and harsh way, which
also satisfied some personal enmities, it was stopped.
We may put aside for good the charge on which he was
condemned, and which in words he admitted, of being
corrupt as a judge. His real fault, and it was a great
one, was that he did not in time open his eyes to the
wrongness and evil, patent to every one, and to himself
as soon as pointed out, of the traditional fashion in his
court of eking out by irregular gifts the salary of such an
office as his.

Thus Bacon was condemned both to suffering and to
dishonour; and, as has been observed, condemned without a trial. But it must also be observed, that it was
entirely owing to his own act that he had not a trial, and
with a trial the opportunity of cross-examining witnesses
and of explaining openly the matters urged against him.
The proceedings in the Lords were preliminary to the
trial: when the time came, Bacon, of his own choice,
stopped them from going further by his confession and
submission.   Considering the view which he claimed
to take of his own case, his behaviour was wanting in
courage and spirit. From the moment that the attack

L

on him shifted from a charge of authorising illegal
monopolies to a charge of personal corruption, he never
fairly met his accusers. The distress and anxiety, no
doubt, broke down his health ; and twice, when he was
called upon to be in his place in the House of Lords, he
was obliged to excuse himself on the ground that he was
too ill to leave his bed. But between the time of the
first charge and his condemnation seven weeks elapsed :
and though he was able to go down to Gorhambury, he
never in that time showed himself in the House of Lords.
Whether or not, while the Committees were busy in
collecting the charges, he would have been allowed to take
part, to put questions to the witnesses, or to produce his
own, he never attempted to do so ; and by the course he
took there was no other opportunity. To have stood his
trial could hardly have increased his danger, or aggravated his punishment; and it would only have been
worthy of his name and place, if not to have made a
fight for his character and integrity, at least to have
bravely said what he had made up his mind to admit,
and what no one could have said more nobly and
pathetically, in open Parliament. But he was cowed
at the fierceness of the disapprobation, manifest in both
Houses. He shrunk from looking his peers and his
judges in the face. His friends obtained for him that
he should not be brought to the bar, and that all should
pass in writing. But they saved his dignity at the expense
of his substantial reputation. The observation that the
charges against him were not sifted by cross-examination
applies equally to his answers to them. The allegations
of both sides would have come down to us in a more
trustworthy shape if the case had gone on. But to give

up the struggle, and to escape by any humiliation from
a regular public trial, seems to have been his only
thought, when he found that the King and Buckingham
could not or would not save him.

But the truth is that he knew that a trial of this kind
was a trial only in name. He knew that when a charge
of this sort was brought, it was not meant to be really in-
vestigated in open court, but to be driven home by proofs
carefully prepared beforehand, against which the accused
had little chance. He knew, too, that in those days to
resist in earnest an accusation was apt to be taken as an
insult to the court which entertained it. And further,
for the prosecutor to accept a submission and confession
without pushing to the formality of a public trial, and
therefore a public exposure, was a favour. It was a
favour which by his advice, as against the King's honour,
had been refused to Suffolk ; it was a favour which, in
a much lighter charge, had by his advice been refused
to his colleague Yelverton only a few months before,
when Bacon, in sentencing him, took occasion to expatiate
on the heinous guilt of misprisions or mistakes in men
in high places. The humiliation was not complete without the trial, but it was for humiliation and not fair investigation that the trial was wanted. Bacon knew that
the trial would only prolong his agony, and give a further
triumph to his enemies.

That there was any plot against Bacon, and much more
that Buckingham to save himself was a party to it, is of
course absurd. Buckingham, indeed, was almost the only
man in the Lords who said anything for Bacon, and,
alone, he voted against his punishment. But considering what Buckingham was, and what he dared to do

when he pleased, he was singularly cool in helping Bacon.
Williams, the astute Dean of Westminster, who was to
be Bacon's successor as Lord Keeper, had got his ear, and
advised him not to endanger himself by trying to save
delinquents. He did not. Indeed, as the inquiry went on,
he began to take the high moral ground ; he was shocked
at the Chancellor's conduct ; he would not have believed
that it could have been so bad; his disgrace was richly
deserved. Buckingham kept up appearances by saying
a word for him from time to time in Parliament, which
he knew would be useless, and which he certainly took
no measures to make effective. It is sometimes said that
Buckingham never knew what dissimulation was. He
was capable, at least, of the perfidy and cowardice of
utter selfishness. Bacon's conspicuous fall diverted
men's thoughts from the far more scandalous wickedness
of the great favourite. But though there was no plot,
though the blow fell upon Bacon almost accidentally,
there were many who rejoiced to be able to drive it
home. We can hardly wonder that foremost among
them was Coke. This was the end of the long rivalry
between Bacon and Coke, from the time that Essex
pressed Bacon against Coke in vain, to the day when
Bacon as Chancellor drove Coke from his seat for his
bad law, and as Privy Councillor ordered him to be prosecuted in the Star Chamber for riotously breaking
open men's doors to get his daughter. The two men
thoroughly disliked and undervalued one another. Coke
made light of Bacon's law. Bacon saw clearly Coke's
narrowness and ignorance out of that limited legal sphere
in which he was supposed to know everything, his prejudiced and interested use of his knowledge, his coarse-

ness and insolence. But now in Parliament Coke was
supreme, "our Hercules," as his friends said. He posed
as the enemy of all abuses and corruption. He brought
his unrivalled though not always accurate knowledge of
law and history to the service of the Committees, and
took care that the Chancellor's name should not be forgotten when it could be connected with some bad business
of patent or Chancery abuse. It was the great revenge
of the Common Law on the encroaching and insulting
Chancery which had now proved so foul. And he could
not resist the opportunity of marking the revenge of
professional knowledge over Bacon's airs of philosophical
superiority. "To restore things to their original" was
his sneer in Parliament, "this, *Instauratio Magna.
Instaurare paras :—Instaura leges justitiamque prius.*" [1]

The charge of corruption was as completely a surprise
to Bacon as it was to the rest of the world. And yet,
as soon as the blot was hit, he saw in a moment that his
position was hopeless—he knew that he had been doing
wrong; though all the time he had never apparently
given it a thought, and he insisted, what there is every
reason to believe, that no present had induced him to
give an unjust decision. It was the power of custom
over a character naturally and by habit too pliant to

[1] *Commons' Journals,* iii. 578. In his copy of the *Novum
Organum,* received *ex dono auctoris,* Coke wrote the same words.
        "*Auctori consilium.*
    Instaurare paras veterum documenta sophorum :
    Instaura leges justitiamque prius."
He added, with allusion to the ship in the frontispiece of the
Novum Organum,
            "It deserveth not to be read in schools,
            But to be freighted in the ship of Fools."

circumstances. Custom made him insensible to the
evil of receiving recommendations from Buckingham in
favour of suitors. Custom made him insensible to the
evil of what it seems every one took for granted,—receiving gifts from suitors. In the Court of James I. the
atmosphere which a man in office breathed was loaded
with the taint of gifts and bribes. Presents were as
much the rule, as indispensable for those who hoped to
get on, as they are now in Turkey. Even in Elizabeth's
days, when Bacon was struggling to win her favour, and
was in the greatest straits for money, he borrowed £500
to buy a jewel for the Queen. When he was James's
servant the giving of gifts became a necessity. New
Year's Day brought round its tribute of gold vases and
gold pieces to the King and Buckingham. And this
was the least. Money was raised by the sale of offices
and titles. For £20,000, having previously offered
£10,000 in vain, the Chief-Justice of England, Montague,
became Lord Mandeville and Treasurer. The bribe was
sometimes disguised : a man became a Privy Councillor,
like Cranfield, or a Chief-Justice, like Ley (afterwards
"the good Earl," "unstained with gold or fee," of
Milton's Sonnet), by marrying a cousin or a niece of
Buckingham. When Bacon was made a Peer, he had
also given him "the making of a Baron"; that is to
say, he might raise money by bargaining with some one
who wanted a peerage ; when, however, later on, he
asked Buckingham for a repetition of the favour, Buckingham gave him a lecture on the impropriety of
prodigality, which should make it seem that "while the
King was asking money of Parliament with one hand
he was giving with the other." How things were in

Chancery in the days of the Queen, and of Bacon's predecessors, we know little; but Bacon himself implies that there was nothing new in what he did. " All my lawyers," said James, "are so bred and nursed in corruption that they cannot leave it." Bacon's Chancellorship coincided with the full bloom of Buckingham's favour : and Buckingham set the fashion, beyond all before him, of extravagance in receiving and in spending. Encompassed by such assumptions and such customs, Bacon administered the Chancery. Suitors did there what people did everywhere else ; they acknowledged by a present the trouble they gave, or the benefit they gained. It may be that Bacon's known difficulties about money, his expensive ways and love of pomp, his easiness of nature, his lax discipline over his servants, encouraged this profuseness of giving. And Bacon let it be. He asked no questions ; he knew that he worked hard and well ; he knew that it could go on without affecting his purpose to do justice "from the greatest to the groom." A stronger character, a keener conscience, would have faced the question, not only whether he was not setting the most ruinous of precedents, but whether any man could be so sure of himself as to go on dealing justly with gifts in his hands. But Bacon, who never dared to face the question, what James was, what Buckingham was, let himself be spell-bound by custom. He knew in the abstract that judges ought to have nothing to do with gifts, and had said so impressively in his charges to them. Yet he went on self-complacent, secure, almost innocent, building up a great tradition of corruption in the very heart of English justice, till the challenge of Parliament, which began in him its terrible

and relentless but most unequal prosecution of justice
against ministers who had betrayed the commonwealth in
serving the Crown, woke him from his dream, and made
him see, as others saw it, the guilt of a great judge who,
under whatever extenuating pretext, allowed the suspicion
to arise that he might sell justice. "In the midst of a state
of as great affliction as mortal man can endure," he wrote
to the Lords of the Parliament, in making his submission,
—"I shall begin with the professing gladness in some
things. The first is that hereafter the greatness of a
judge or magistrate shall be no sanctuary or protection
of guiltiness, which is the beginning of a golden world.
The next, that after this example it is like that judges
will fly from anything that is in the likeness of corruption as from a serpent." Bacon's own judgment on
himself, deliberately repeated, is characteristic, and probably comes near the truth. "Howsoever I acknowledge
the sentence just and for reformation's sake fit," he
writes to Buckingham from the Tower, where, for form's
sake, he was imprisoned for a few miserable days, he
yet had been "the justest Chancellor that hath been in
the five changes that have been since Sir Nicolas Bacon's
time." He repeated the same thing yet more deliberately in later times. "*I was the justest judge that was in
England these fifty years. But it was the justest censure in
Parliament that was these two hundred years.*"

He might have gone on to add, "the Wisest Counsellor; and yet none on whom rested heavier blame;
none of whom England might more justly complain."
Good counsels given, submissive acquiescence in the
worst, — this is the history of his statesmanship.
Bacon, whose eye was everywhere, was not sparing of

his counsels. On all the great questions of the time he
has left behind abundant evidence, not only of what he
thought, but of what he advised. And in every case
these memorials are marked with the insight, the independence, the breadth of view, and the moderation of
a mind which is bent on truth. He started, of course,
from a basis which we are now hardly able to understand
or allow for, the idea of absolute royal power and prerogative which James had enlarged and hardened out
of the Kingship of the Tudors, itself imperious and
arbitrary enough, but always seeking, with a tact of
which James was incapable, to be in touch and sympathy
with popular feeling. But it was a basis which in principle every one of any account as yet held or professed
to hold, and which Bacon himself held on grounds of
philosophy and reason. He could see no hope for orderly
and intelligent government except in a ruler whose
wisdom had equal strength to assert itself ; and he
looked down with incredulity and scorn on the notion
of anything good coming out of what the world then
knew or saw of popular opinion or parliamentary government. But when it came to what was wise and fitting
for absolute power to do, in the way of general measures
and policy, he was for the most part right. He saw the
inexorable and pressing necessity of putting the finance
of the kingdom on a safe footing. He saw the necessity
of a sound and honest policy in Ireland. He saw the
mischief of the Spanish alliance in spite of his curious
friendship with Gondomar, and detected the real and
increasing weakness of the Spanish monarchy, which still
awed mankind. He saw the growing danger of abuses
in Church and State which were left untouched, and

were protected by the punishment of those who dared
to complain of them. He saw the confusion and injustice
of much of that common law of which the lawyers were
so proud ; and would have attempted, if he had been
able, to emulate Justinian, and anticipate the Code
Napoleon, by a rational and consistent digest. Above
all, he never ceased to impress on James the importance,
and, if wisely used, the immense advantages, of his Parliaments. Himself, for great part of his life, an active and
popular member of the House of Commons, he saw that
not only it was impossible to do without it, but that if
fairly, honourably, honestly dealt with, it would become
a source of power and confidence which would double the
strength of the Government both at home and abroad.
Yet of all this wisdom nothing came. The finance of the
kingdom was still ruined by extravagance and corruption
in a time of rapidly-developing prosperity and wealth.
The wounds of Ireland were unhealed. It was neither
peace nor war with Spain, and hot infatuation for its
friendship alternated with cold fits of distrust and
estrangement. Abuses flourished and multiplied under
great patronage. The King's one thought about Parliament was how to get as much money out of it as he
could, with as little other business as possible. Bacon's
counsels were the prophecies of Cassandra in that so
prosperous but so disastrous reign. All that he did was
to lend the authority of his presence, in James's most
intimate counsels, to policy and courses of which he
saw the unwisdom and the perils. James and Buckingham made use of him when they wanted. But they
would have been very different in their measures and
their statesmanship if they had listened to him.

Mirabeau said, what of course had been said before him, "On ne vaut, dans la partie exécutive de la vie humaine, que par le caractère." This is the key to Bacon's failures as a judge and as a statesman; and why, knowing so much more and judging so much more wisely than James and Buckingham, he must be identified with the misdoings of that ignoble reign. He had the courage of his opinions, but a man wants more than that; he needs the manliness and the public spirit to enforce them, if they are true and salutary. But this is what Bacon had not. He did not mind being rebuffed; he knew that he was right, and did not care. But to stand up against the King, to contradict him after he had spoken, to press an opinion or a measure on a man whose belief in his own wisdom was infinite, to risk not only being set down as a dreamer, but the King's displeasure, and the ruin of being given over to the will of his enemies, this Bacon had not the fibre, or the stiffness, or the self-assertion to do. He did not do what a man of firm will and strength of purpose, a man of high integrity, of habitual resolution, would have done. Such men insist when they are responsible, and when they know that they are right; and they prevail, or accept the consequences. Bacon, knowing all that he did, thinking all that he thought, was content to be the echo and the instrument of the cleverest, the foolishest, the vainest, the most pitiably unmanly of English kings.

CHAPTER VII.

THE tremendous sentences of those days, with their crushing fines, were often worse in sound than in reality. They meant that for the moment a man was defeated and disgraced. But it was quite understood that it did not necessarily follow that they would be enforced in all their severity. The fine might be remitted; the imprisonment shortened; the ban of exclusion taken off. At another turn of events or caprice, the man himself might return to favour, and take his place in Parliament or the Council, as if nothing had happened. But, of course, a man might have powerful enemies, and the sentence might be pressed. His fine might be assigned to some favourite; and he might be ruined, even if in the long run he was pardoned; or he might remain indefinitely a prisoner. Raleigh had remained to perish at last in dishonour. Northumberland, Raleigh's fellow-prisoner, after fifteen years' captivity, was released this year. The year after Bacon's condemnation such criminals as Lord and Lady Somerset were released from the Tower, after a six years' imprisonment. Southampton, the accomplice of Essex, Suffolk, sentenced as late as 1619 by Bacon for embezzlement, sat in the House of Peers which judged Bacon, and both of them took a prominent part in judging him.

To Bacon the sentence was ruinous. It proved an irretrievable overthrow as regards public life, and though some parts of it were remitted, and others lightened, it plunged his private affairs into trouble which weighed heavily on him for his few remaining years. To his deep distress and horror he had to go to the Tower to satisfy the terms of his sentence. "Good my Lord," he writes to Buckingham, May 31, "procure my warrant for my discharge this day. Death is so far from being unwelcome to me, as I have called for it as far as Christian resolution would permit any time these two months. But to die before the time of his Majesty's grace, in this disgraceful place, is even the worst that could be." He was released after two or three days, and he thanks Buckingham (June 4) for getting him out to do him and the King faithful service—" wherein, by the grace of God, your Lordship shall find that my adversity hath neither *spent* nor *pent* my spirits." In the autumn his fine was remitted ; that is, it was assigned to persons nominated by Bacon, who, as the Crown had the first claim on all his goods, served as a protection against his other creditors, who were many and some of them clamorous ; and it was followed by his pardon. His successor, Williams, now Bishop of Lincoln, who stood in great fear of Parliament, tried to stop the pardon. The assignment of the fine, he said to Buckingham, was a gross job : "it is much spoken against, not for the matter (for no man objects to that), but for the manner, which is full of knavery, and a wicked precedent. For by this assignment he is protected from all his

creditors, which (I dare say) was neither his Majesty's
nor your Lordship's meaning." It was an ill-natured
and cowardly piece of official pedantry, to plunge deeper
a drowning man: but in the end the pardon was passed.
It does not appear whether Buckingham interfered to
overrule the Lord Keeper's scruples. Buckingham was
certainly about this time very much out of humour with
Bacon, for a reason which, more than anything else,
discloses the deep meanness which lurked under his show
of magnanimity and pride. He had chosen this moment
to ask Bacon for York House. This meant that Bacon
would never more want it. Even Bacon was stung by
such a request to a friend in his condition, and declined
to part with it: and Buckingham accordingly was
offended, and made Bacon feel it. Indeed, there is
reason to think with Mr. Spedding that for the sealing
of his pardon Bacon was indebted to the good offices
with the King, not of Buckingham, but of the Spaniard,
Gondomar, with whom Bacon had always been on terms
of cordiality and respect, and who at this time certainly
" brought about something on his behalf, which his
other friends either had not dared to attempt, or had
not been able to obtain."

But though Bacon had his pardon, he had not
received permission to come within the verge of the
Court, which meant that he could not live in London.
His affairs were in great disorder, his health was bad,
and he was cut off from books. He wrote an appeal
to the Peers who had condemned him, asking them
to intercede with the King for the enlargement of
his liberty. "I am old," he wrote, "weak, ruined, in
want, a very subject of pity." The Tower at least gave

him the neighbourhood of those who could help him. "There I could have company, physicians, conference with my creditors and friends about my debts and the necessities of my estate, helps for my studies and the writings I have in hand. Here I live upon the sword-point of a sharp air, endangered if I go abroad, dulled if I stay within, solitary and comfortless, without company, banished from all opportunities to treat with any to do myself good, and to help out my wrecks." If the Lords would recommend his suit to the King, "You shall do a work of charity and nobility, you shall do me good, you shall do my creditors good, and it may be you shall do posterity good, if out of the carcase of dead and rotten greatness (as out of Samson's lion) there may be honey gathered for the use of future times." But Parliament was dissolved before the touching appeal reached them; and Bacon had to have recourse to other expedients. He consulted Selden about the technical legality of the sentence. He appealed to Buckingham, who vouchsafed to appear more placable. Once more he had recourse to Gondomar, "in that solitude of friends, which is the base-court of adversity," as a man whom he had "observed to have the magnanimity of his own nation, and the cordiality of ours, and I am sure, the wit of both,"—and who had been equally kind to him in "both his fortunes"; and he proposed through Gondomar to present Gorhambury to Buckingham "for nothing," as a peace-offering. But the purchase of his liberty was to come in another way. Bacon had reconciled himself to giving up York House; but now Buckingham would not have it: he had found another house, he said, which suited him as well. That

is to say, he did not now choose to have York House
from Bacon himself; but he meant to have it. Accordingly, Buckingham let Bacon know through a friend of
Bacon's, Sir Edward Sackville, that the price of his liberty
to live in London was the cession of York House—not
to Buckingham, but of all men in the world, to Lionel
Cranfield, the man who had been so bitter against Bacon
in the House of Commons. This is Sir Edward Sackville's account to Bacon of his talk with Buckingham ;
it is characteristic of every one concerned :—

"In the forenoon he laid the law, but in the afternoon he
preached the gospel ; when, after some revivations of the old dis-
taste concerning York House, he most nobly opened his heart unto
me ; wherein I read that which augured much good towards you.
After which revelation the book was again sealed up, and must in
his own time only by himself be again manifested unto you. I
have leave to remember some of the vision, and am not forbidden
to write it. He vowed (not court like), but constantly to appear
your friend so much, as if his Majesty should abandon the care of
you, you should share his fortune with him. He pleased to tell me
how much he had been beholden to you, how well he loved you,
how unkindly he took the denial of your house (for so he will needs
understand it) ; but the close for all this was harmonious, since he
protested he would seriously begin to study your ends, now that
the world should see he had no ends on you. He is in hand with
the work, and therefore will by no means accept of your offer,
though I can assure you the tender hath much won upon him, and
mellowed his heart towards you, and your genius directed you
aright when you writ that letter of denial to the Duke. The King
saw it, and all the rest, which made him say unto the Marquis, you
played an after-game well ; and that now he had no reason to be
much offended.

"I have already talked of the Revelation, and now am to speak
in apocalyptical language, which I hope you will rightly comment :
whereof if you make difficulty, the bearer can help you with the
key of the cypher.

"My Lord Falkland by this time hath showed you London from

Highgate. *If York House were gone, the town were yours,* and all your straitest shackles clean off, besides more comfort than the city air only. The Marquis would be exceeding glad the Treasurer had it. This I know ; yet this you must not know from me. Bargain with him presently, upon as good conditions as you can procure, so you have direct motion from the Marquis to let him have it. Seem not to dive into the secret of it, though you are purblind if you see not through it. I have told Mr. Meautys how I would wish your Lordship now to make an end of it. From him I beseech you take it, and from me only the advice to perform it. If you part not speedily with it, you may defer the good which is approaching near you, and disappointing other aims (which must either shortly receive content or never), perhaps anew yield matter of discontent, though you maybe indeed as innocent as before. Make the Treasurer believe that since the Marquis will by no means accept of it, and that you must part with it, you are more willing to pleasure him than anybody else, because you are given to understand my Lord Marquis so inclines ; which inclination, if the Treasurer shortly send unto you about it, desire may be more clearly manifested than as yet it hath been ; since as I remember none hitherto hath told you *in terminis terminantibus* that the Marquis desires you should gratify the Treasurer. I know that way the hare runs, and that my Lord Marquis longs until Cranfield hath it ; and so I wish too, for your good; yet would not it were absolutely passed until my Lord Marquis did send or write unto you to let him have it ; for then his so disposing of it were but the next degree removed from the immediate acceptance of it, and your Lordship freed from doing it otherwise than to please him, and to comply with his own will and way."

It need hardly be said that when Cranfield got it, it soon passed into Buckingham's hands. "Bacon consented to part with his house, and Buckingham in return consented to give him his liberty." Yet Bacon could write to him, "low as I am, I had rather sojourn in a college in Cambridge than recover a good fortune by any other but yourself." "As for York House," he bids Toby Matthews to let Buckingham know, "that *whether in a*

M

straight line or a compass line, I meant it for his Lordship, in the way which I thought might please him best." But liberty did not mean either money or recovered honour. All his life long he had made light of being in debt ; but since his fall this was no longer a condition easy to bear. He had to beg some kind of pension of the King. He had to beg of Buckingham ; " a small matter for my debts would do me more good now than double a twelvemonth hence. I have lost six thousand by the year, besides caps and courtesies. Two things I may assure your Lordship. The one, that I shall lead such a course of life as whatsoever the King doth for me shall rather sort to his Majesty's and your Lordship's honour than to envy : the other, that whatsoever men talk, I can play the good husband, and the King's bounty shall not be lost."

It might be supposed from the tone of these applications that Bacon's mind was bowed down and crushed by the extremity of his misfortune. Nothing could be farther from the truth. In his behaviour during his accusation there was little trace of that high spirit and fortitude shown by far inferior men under like disasters. But the moment the tremendous strain of his misfortunes was taken off, the vigour of his mind recovered itself. The buoyancy of his hopefulness, the elasticity of his energy, are as remarkable as his profound depression. When the end was approaching his thoughts turned at once to other work to be done, ready in plan, ready to be taken up and finished. At the close of his last desperate letter to the King he cannot resist finishing at once with a jest, and with the prospect of two great literary under-takings—

"This is my last suit which I shall make to your Majesty in this business, prostrating myself at your mercy seat, after fifteen years service, wherein I have served your Majesty in my poor endeavours with an entire heart, and, as I presumed to say unto your Majesty, am still a virgin for matters that concern your person and crown ; and now only craving that after eight steps of honour I be not precipitated altogether. But because he that hath taken bribes is apt to give bribes, I will go furder, and present your Majesty with a bribe. For if your Majesty will give me peace and leisure, and God give me life, I will present your Majesty with a good history of England, and a better digest of your laws."

The Tower did, indeed, to use a word of the time, "mate" him. But the moment he was out of it, his quick and fertile mind was immediately at work in all directions, reaching after all kinds of plans, making proof of all kinds of expedients to retrieve the past, arranging all kinds of work according as events might point out the way. His projects for history, for law, for philosophy, for letters, occupy quite as much of his thoughts, as his pardon and his debts ; and they, we have seen, occupied a good deal. If he was pusillanimous in the moment of the storm, his spirit, his force, his varied interests, returned the moment the storm was past. His self-reliance, which was boundless, revived. He never allowed himself to think, however men of his own time might judge him, that the future world would mistake him. "*Aliquis fui inter vivos*," he writes to Gondomar, "*neque omnino intermoriar apud posteros.*" Even in his time he did not give up the hope of being restored to honour and power. He compared himself to Demosthenes, to Cicero, to Seneca, to Marcus Livius, who had been condemned for corrupt dealings as he had been, and had all recovered favour and position. Lookers-on were puzzled and shocked. "He has,"

writes Chamberlain, "no manner of feeling of his fall,
but continuing vain and idle in all his humours as when
he was at the highest." "I am said," Bacon himself
writes, "to have a feather in my head."

Men were mistaken. His thoughts were, for the
moment, more than ever turned to the future ; but he
had not given up hope of having a good deal to say yet
to the affairs of the present. Strangely enough, as it
seems to us, in the very summer after that fatal spring
of 1621 the King called for his opinion concerning the
reformation of Courts of Justice ; and Bacon, just sentenced for corruption and still unpardoned, proceeds
to give his advice as if he were a Privy Counsellor
in confidential employment. Early in the following
year he, according to his fashion, surveyed his position,
and drew up a paper of memoranda, like the notes of
the *Commentarius Solutus* of 1608, about points to be
urged to the King at an interview. Why should not
the King employ him again ? " Your Majesty never chid
me ; " and as to his condemnation, "as the fault was
not against your Majesty, so my fall was not your act."
"Therefore," he goes on, "if your Majesty do at any
time find it fit for your affairs to employ me publicly
upon the stage, I shall so live and spend my time as
neither discontinuance shall disable me nor adversity
shall discourage me, nor anything that I do give any
new scandal or envy upon me." He insists very strongly
that the King's service never miscarried in his hands,
for he simply carried out the King's wise counsels.
" That his Majesty's business never miscarried in my
hands I do not impute to any extraordinary ability in
myself, but to my freedom from any particular, either

friends or ends, and my careful receipt of his directions, being, as I have formerly said to him, but as a bucket and cistern to that fountain—a bucket to draw forth, a cistern to preserve." He is not afraid of the apparent slight to the censure passed on him by Parliament. " For envy, it is an almanack of the old year, and as a friend of mine said, *Parliament died penitent towards me.*" "What the King bestows on me will be further seen than on Paul's steeple." " There be mountebanks, as well in the civil body, as in the natural ; I ever served his Majesty with modesty ; no shouting, no undertaking." In the odd fashion of the time, a fashion in which no one more delighted than himself, he lays hold of sacred words to give point to his argument.

" I may allude to the three petitions of the Litany—*Libera nos Domine ; parce nobis, Domine ; exaudi nos, Domine.* In the first, I am persuaded that his Majesty had a mind to do it, and could not conveniently in respect of his affairs. In the second, he hath done it in my fine and pardon. In the third, he hath likewise performed, in restoring to the light of his countenance."

But if the King did not see fit to restore him to public employment, he would be ready to give private counsel; and he would apply himself to any "literary province " that the King appointed. "I am like ground fresh. If I be left to myself I will graze and bear natural philosophy ; but if the King will plough me up again, and sow me with anything, I hope to give him some yield." "Your Majesty hath power; I have faith. Therefore a miracle may be wrought." And he proposes, for matters in which his pen might be useful, first, as " active " works, the recompiling of laws ; the disposing of wards, and generally the education of youth ; the

regulation of the jurisdiction of Courts; and the regulation of Trade : and for "contemplative," the continuation
of the history of Henry VIII.; a general treatise *de
Legibus et Justitia;* and the "Holy War," against the
Ottomans.

When he wrote this he had already shown what his
unquelled energy could accomplish.   In the summer
and autumn after his condemnation, amid all the worries
and inconveniences of that time, moving about from
place to place, without his books, and without free access
to papers and records, he had written his *History of
Henry VII.*   The theme had, no doubt, been long in
his head.   But the book was the first attempt at philosophical history in the language, and it at once takes
rank with all that the world had yet seen, in classical
times and more recently in Italy, of such history.   He
sent the book, among other persons, to the Queen of
Bohemia, with a phrase, the translation of a trite Latin
commonplace, which may have been the parent of one
which became famous in our time ; and with an expression of absolute confidence in the goodness of his own
work.

"I have read in books that it is accounted a great bliss for a
man to have *Leisure with Honour.*   That was never my fortune.
For time was, I had Honour without Leisure ; and now I have
Leisure without Honour. . . . But my desire is now to have *Leisure
without Loitering*, and not to become an abbey-lubber, as the old
proverb was, but to yield some fruit of my private life. . . . If
King Henry were alive again, I hope verily he would not be so
angry with me for not flattering him, as well pleased in seeing
himself so truly described in colours that will last and be believed."

But the tide had turned against him for good.   A few

fair words, a few grudging doles of money to relieve his
pressing wants, and those sometimes intercepted and
perhaps never rightly granted from an Exchequer which
even Cranfield's finance could not keep filled, were all the
graces that descended upon him from those fountains of
goodness in which he professed to trust with such boundless faith.   The King did not want him, perhaps did not
trust him, perhaps did not really like him.   When the
Novum Organum came out all that he had to say about it
was in the shape of a profane jest that "it was like
the peace of God—it passed all understanding."   Other
men had the ear of Buckingham ; shrewd practical men
of business like Cranfield, who hated Bacon's loose and
careless ways, or the clever ecclesiastic Williams, whose
counsel had steered Buckingham safely through the tempest that wrecked Bacon, and who, with no legal training,
had been placed in Bacon's seat.   "I thought," said
Bacon, "that I should have known my successor."   Williams, for his part, charged Bacon with trying to cheat
his creditors, when his fine was remitted.   With no open
quarrel, Bacon's relations to Buckingham became more
ceremonious and guarded ; the "My singular good Lord"
of the former letters becomes, now that Buckingham had
risen so high and Bacon had sunk so low, "Excellent
Lord."   The one friend to whom Bacon had once wished
to owe everything, had become the great man, now only
to be approached with "sweet meats" and elaborate
courtesy.   But it was no use.   His full pardon Bacon did
not get, though earnestly suing for it, that he might not
"die in ignominy."   He never sat again in Parliament.
The Provostship of Eton fell vacant, and Bacon's hopes
were kindled.   "It were a pretty cell for my fortune.

The College and School I do not doubt but I shall make
to flourish." But Buckingham had promised it to some
nameless follower, and by some process of exchange it
went to Sir Henry Wotton. His English history was
offered in vain. His digest of the Laws was offered in
vain. In vain he wrote a memorandum on the regulation
of usury; notes of advice to Buckingham; elaborate
reports and notes of speeches about a war with Spain,
when that for a while loomed before the country. In
vain he affected an interest which he could hardly have
felt in the Spanish marriage, and the escapade of Buckingham and Prince Charles, which "began," he wrote,
"like a fable of the poets, but deserved all in a piece a
worthy narration." In vain, when the Spanish marriage
was off and the French was on, he proposed to offer to
Buckingham "his service to live a summer as upon mine
own delight at Paris, to settle a fast intelligence between
France and us;" "I have somewhat of the French," he
said, "I love birds, as the King doth." Public patronage
and public employment were at an end for him. His
petitions to the King and Buckingham ceased to be for
office, but for the clearing of his name, and for the means
of living. It is piteous to read the earnestness of his
requests. "Help me (dear Sovereign lord and master),
pity me so far as that I who have borne a bag be not
now in my age forced in effect to bear a wallet." The
words are from a carefully-prepared and rhetorical letter
which was not sent, but they express what he added to
a letter presenting the *De Augmentis; "det Vestra Majestas
obolum Belisario."* Again, "I prostrate myself at your Majesty's feet; I your ancient servant, now sixty-four years
old in age, and three years and five months old in misery.

I desire not from your Majesty means, nor place, nor
employment, but only after so long a time of expiation,
a complete and total remission of the sentence of the
Upper House, to the end that blot of ignominy may be
removed from me and from my memory and posterity,
that I die not a condemned man, but may be to your
Majesty, as I am to God, *nova creatura.*" But the pardon
never came. Sir John Bennett, who had been condemned
as a corrupt judge by the same Parliament, and between
whose case and Bacon's there was as much difference,
"I will not say as between black and white, but as between black and grey," had got his full pardon, "and
they say shall sit in Parliament." Lord Suffolk had been
one of Bacon's judges. "I hope I deserve not to be the
only outcast." But whether the Court did not care, or
whether, as he once suspected, there was some old enemy
like Coke, who "had a tooth against him," and was
watching any favour shown him, he died without his
wish being fulfilled, "to live out of want and to die out
of ignominy."

Bacon was undoubtedly an impoverished man, and
straitened in his means; but this must be understood as
in relation to the rank and position which he still held,
and the work which he wanted done for the *Instauratio.*
His will, dated a few months before his death, shows
that it would be a mistake to suppose that he was in
penury. He no doubt often wanted ready money, and
might be vexed by creditors. But he kept a large
household, and was able to live in comfort at Gray's
Inn or at Gorhambury. A man who speaks in his will
of his "four coach geldings and his best caroache,"
besides many legacies, and who proposes to found two

lectures at the universities, may have troubles about
debts and be cramped in his expenditure; but it is only
relatively to his station that he can be said to be poor.
And to subordinate officers of the Treasury who kept
him out of his rights, he could still write a sharp letter,
full of his old force and edge. A few months before his
death he thus wrote to the Lord Treasurer Ley, who
probably had made some difficulty about a claim for
money :—

"My Lord—I humbly entreat your Lordship, and (if I may use
the word) advise your Lordship to make me a better answer. Your
Lordship is interessed in honour, in the opinion of all that hear how
I am dealt with. If your Lordship malice me for Long's cause,
surely it was one of the justest businesses that ever was in Chancery.
I will avouch it; and how deeply I was tempted therein, your
Lordship knoweth best. Your Lordship may do well to think of
your grave as I do of mine; and to beware of hardness of heart.
And as for fair words, it is a wind by which neither your Lordship
nor any man else can sail long. Howsoever, I am the man that
shall give all due respects and reverence to your great place.
    "20th June 1625.   Fr. St. Alban."

Bacon always claimed that he was not "vindicative."
But considering how Bishop Williams, when he was
Lord Keeper, had charged Bacon with "knavery" and
"deceiving his creditors" in the arrangements about his
fine, it is not a little strange to find that at the end of
his life Bacon had so completely made friends with him
that he chose him as the person to whom he meant to
leave his speeches and letters, which he was "willing
should not be lost," and also the charge of superintending
two foundations of £200 a year for Natural Science at
the universities. And the Bishop accepted the charge.
The end of this, one of the most pathetic of histories,

was at hand ; the end was not the less pathetic because it
came in so homely a fashion. On a cold day in March,
he stopped his coach in the snow on his way to Highgate,
to try the effect of cold in arresting putrefaction. He
bought a hen from a woman by the way, and stuffed it
with snow. He was taken with a bad chill, which forced
him to stop at a strange house, Lord Arundel's, to whom
he wrote his last letter, a letter of apology for using
his house. He did not write the letter as a dying
man. But disease had fastened on him. A few days
after, early on Easter morning, April 9th, 1626, he passed
away. He was buried at St. Albans, in the Church of
St. Michael, "the only Christian church within the walls
of old Verulam." "For my name and memory," he
said in his will, "I leave it to men's charitable speeches,
and to foreign nations, and the next ages." So he
died : the brightest, richest, largest mind but one, in the
age which had seen Shakespeare and his fellows ; so
bright and rich and large that there have been found
those who identify him with the writer of *Hamlet* and
Othello. That is idle. Bacon could no more have written
the plays than Shakespeare could have prophesied the
triumphs of natural philosophy. So ended a career, than
which no other in his time had grander and nobler aims,
aims, however mistaken, for the greatness and good of
England, aims for the enlargement of knowledge and
truth, and for the benefit of mankind. So ended a career
which had mounted slowly and painfully, but resolutely,
to the highest pinnacle of greatness, greatness full of
honour and beneficent activity, suddenly to plunge down
to depths where honour and hope were irrecoverable. So
closed, in disgrace and disappointment and neglect, the

last sad chapter of a life which had begun so brightly,
which had achieved such permanent triumphs, which had
lost itself so often in the tangles of insincerity and evil
custom, which was disfigured and marred by great misfortunes and still more by great mistakes of his own,
which was in many ways misunderstood not only by his
generation but by himself, but which he left in the constant and almost unaccountable faith that it would be
understood and greatly honoured by posterity.   With
all its glories, it was the greatest shipwreck, the greatest
tragedy, of an age which saw many.

But in these gloomy and dreary days of depression
and vain hope to which his letters bear witness—"three
years and five months old in misery," again later, "a
long cleansing week of five years' expiation and more"—
his interest in his great undertaking and his industry
never flagged.   The King did not want what he offered,
did not want his histories, did not want his help about
law.   Well, then, he had work of his own on which his
heart was set; and if the King did not want his time,
he had the more for himself.   Even in the busy days of
his Chancellorship he had prepared and carried through
the press the *Novum Organum*, which he published on the
very eve of his fall.   It was one of those works which
quicken a man's powers, and prove to him what he can
do; and it had its effect.   His mind was never more alert
than in these years of adversity, his labour never more
indefatigable, his powers of expression never more keen
and versatile and strong.   Besides the political writings
of grave argument for which he found time, these five
years teem with the results of work.   In the year before
his death he sketched out once more, in a letter to a

Venetian correspondent, Fra Fulgenzio, the friend of
Sarpi, the plan of his great work, on which he was still
busy, though with fast diminishing hopes of seeing it
finished. To another foreign correspondent, a professor
of philosophy at Annecy, and a distinguished mathemati-
cian, Father Baranzan, who had raised some questions
about Bacon's method, and had asked what was to be
done with metaphysics, he wrote in eager acknowledgment of the interest which his writings had excited, and
insisting on the paramount necessity, above everything, of
the observation of facts and of natural history, out of
which philosophy may be built. But the most comprehensive view of his intellectual projects in all directions, "the
fullest account of his own personal feelings and designs
as a writer which we have from his own pen," is given
in a letter to the venerable friend of his early days,
Bishop Andrewes, who died a few months after him.
Part, he says, of his *Instauratio*, "the work in mine own
judgement (*si nunquam fallit imago*) I do most esteem,"
has been published : but because he "doubts that it
flies too high over men's heads," he proposes " to draw it
down to the sense " by examples of Natural History.
He has enlarged and translated the *Advancement* into
the *De Augmentis*.   "Because he could not altogether
desert the civil person that he had borne," he had begun
a work on Laws, intermediate between philosophical
jurisprudence and technical law.   He had hoped to com-
pile a digest of English law, but found it more than he
could do alone, and had laid it aside.   The *Instauratio*
had contemplated the good of men "in the dowries of
nature :" the *Laws*, their good "in society and the
dowries of government."   As he owed duty to his

country, and could no longer do it service, he meant to
do it honour by his history of Henry VII. His *Essays*
were but "recreations;" and remembering that all his
writings had hitherto "gone all into the City and none
into the Temple," he wished to make "some poor
oblation," and therefore had chosen an argument mixed
of religious and civil considerations, the dialogue of
"an Holy War" against the Ottoman, which he never
finished, but which he intended to dedicate to Andrewes,
"in respect of our ancient and private acquaintance, and
because amongst the men of our times I hold you in
special reverence."

The question naturally presents itself, in regard to a
friend of Bishop Andrewes, what was Bacon as regards
religion? And the answer, it seems to me, can admit of
no doubt. The obvious and superficial thing to say is
that his religion was but an official one, a tribute to custom and opinion. But it was not so. Both in his philosophical thinking, and in the feelings of his mind in the
various accidents and occasions of life, Bacon was a
religious man, with a serious and genuine religion. His
sense of the truth and greatness of religion was as real
as his sense of the truth and greatness of nature; they
were interlaced together, and could not be separated,
though they were to be studied separately and inde-
pendently. The call, repeated through all his works
from the earliest to the last, *Da Fidei quæ Fidei sunt*,
was a warning against confusing the two, but was an
earnest recognition of the claims of each. The solemn
religious words in which his prefaces and general statements often wind up with thanksgiving and hope and
prayer, are no mere words of course; they breathe the

spirit of the deepest conviction.   It is true that he takes
the religion of Christendom as he finds it.   The grounds
of belief, the relation of faith to reason, the profounder
inquiries into the basis of man's knowledge of the
Eternal and Invisible, are out of the circle within which
he works.   What we now call the philosophy of religion
is absent from his writings.   In truth, his mind was not
qualified to grapple with such questions.   There is no
sign in his writings that he ever tried his strength
against them ; that he ever cared to go below the surface
into the hidden things of mind and what mind deals
with above and beyond sense—those metaphysical difficulties and depths, as we call them, which there is no
escaping, and which are as hard to explore and as dangerous to mistake as the forces and combinations of
external nature.   But it does not follow, because he had
not asked all the questions that others have asked, that
he had not thought out his reasonable faith.   His religion was not one of mere vague sentiment ; it was the
result of reflection and deliberate judgment.   It was
the discriminating and intelligent Church of England
religion of Hooker and Andrewes, which had gone back
to something deeper and nobler in Christianity than
the popular Calvinism of the earlier Reformation ; and
though sternly hostile to the system of the Papacy, both
on religious and political grounds, attempted to judge it
with knowledge and justice.   This deliberate character
of his belief is shown in the remarkable Confession of
Faith which he left behind him : a closely-reasoned and
nobly-expressed survey of Christian theology—" a *sum-
ma theologiæ*, digested into seven pages of the finest
English of the days when its tones were finest."   "The

entire scheme of Christian theology," as Mr. Spedding
says, "is constantly in his thoughts; underlies everything; defines for him the limits of human speculation;
and, as often as the course of inquiry touches at any
point the boundary line, never fails to present itself.
There is hardly any occasion or any kind of argument
into which it does not at one time or another incidentally
introduce itself." Doubtless it was a religion which in
him was compatible, as it has been in others, with
grave faults of temperament and character. But it is
impossible to doubt that it was honest, that it elevated
his thoughts, that it was a refuge and stay in the times
of trouble.

CHAPTER VIII.

BACON'S PHILOSOPHY.

BACON was one of those men to whom posterity forgives a great deal, for the greatness of what he has done and attempted for posterity. It is idle, unless all honest judgment is foregone, to disguise the many deplorable shortcomings of his life; it is unjust to have one measure for him, and another for those about him and opposed to him. But it is not too much to say that in temper, in honesty, in labour, in humility, in reverence, he was the most perfect example that the world had yet seen of the student of nature, the enthusiast for knowledge. That such a man was tempted and fell, and suffered the Nemesis of his fall, is an instance of the awful truth embodied in the tragedy of *Faust*. But his genuine devotion, so unwearied and so paramount, to a great idea and a great purpose for the good of all generations to come, must shield him from the insult of Pope's famous and shallow epigram. Whatever may have been his sins, and they were many, he cannot have been the "meanest of mankind," who lived and died, holding unaltered, amid temptations and falls, so noble a conception of the use and calling of his life: the duty and service of helping his brethren to know as they had

N

never yet learned to know. That thought never left him ; the obligations it imposed were never forgotten in the crush and heat of business ; the toils, thankless at the time, which it heaped upon him in addition to the burdens of public life, were never refused. Nothing diverted him, nothing made him despair. He was not discouraged because he was not understood. There never was any one in whose life the "*Souveraineté du but*" was more certain and more apparent; and that object was the second greatest that man can have. To teach men to know is only next to making them good.

The Baconian philosophy, the reforms of the *Novum Organum*, the method of experiment and induction, are commonplaces, and sometimes lead to a misconception of what Bacon did. Bacon is, and is not, the founder of modern science. What Bacon believed could be done, what he hoped and divined, for the correction and development of human knowledge, was one thing ; what his methods were, and how far they were successful is another. It would hardly be untrue to say that though Bacon is the parent of modern science, his methods contributed nothing to its actual discoveries; neither by possibility could they have done so. The great and wonderful work which the world owes to him was in the idea, and not in the execution. The idea was that the systematic and wide examination of facts was the first thing to be done in science, and that till this had been done faithfully and impartially, with all the appliances and all the safeguards that experience and forethought could suggest, all generalisations, all anticipations from mere reasoning, must be adjourned and postponed ; and further, that sought on these conditions,

knowledge, certain and fruitful, beyond all that men
then imagined, could be attained. His was the faith of
the discoverer, the imagination of the poet, the voice of
the prophet. But his was not the warrior's arm, the
engineer's skill, the architect's creativeness. "I only
sound the clarion," he says, "but I enter not into the
battle;" and, with a Greek quotation very rare with
him, he compares himself to one of Homer's peaceful
heralds, χαίρετε κήρυκες, Διὸς ἄγγελοι ἠδὲ καὶ ἀνδρῶν.
Even he knew not the full greatness of his own enterprise. He underrated the vastness and the subtlety of
nature. He overrated his own appliances to bring it
under his command. He had not that incommunicable
genius and instinct of the investigator which in such
men as Faraday close hand to hand with phenomena.
His weapons and instruments wanted precision ; they
were powerful up to a certain point, but they had the
clumsiness of an unpractised time. Cowley compared
him to Moses on Pisgah surveying the promised land ;
it was but a distant survey, and Newton was the
Joshua who began to take possession of it.

The idea of the great enterprise, in its essential
outline, and with a full sense of its originality and
importance, was early formed, and was even sketched
on paper with Bacon's characteristic self-reliance when
he was but twenty - five. Looking back, in a letter
written in the last year of his life, on the ardour and
constancy with which he had clung to his faith—"in
that purpose my mind never waxed old, in that long
interval of time it never cooled"—he remarks that it
was then "forty years since he put together a youthful
essay on these matters, which with vast confidence I

called by the high-sounding title, The Greatest Birth of
Time." The "Greatest Birth of Time," whatever it was,
has perished, though the name, altered to "Partus Temporis *Masculus*," has survived, attached to some fragments of uncertain date and arrangement. But in very
truth the child was born, and, as Bacon says, for forty
years grew and developed, with many changes yet the
same. Bacon was most tenacious, not only of ideas, but
even of the phrases, images, and turns of speech in
which they had once flashed on him and taken shape in
his mind. The features of his undertaking remained
the same from first to last, only expanded and enlarged
as time went on and experience widened; his conviction
that the knowledge of nature, and with it the power
to command and to employ nature, were within the
capacity of mankind and might be restored to them; the
certainty that of this knowledge men had as yet acquired
but the most insignificant part, and that all existing
claims to philosophical truth were as idle and precarious
as the guesses and traditions of the vulgar; his belief
that no greater object could be aimed at than to sweep
away once and for ever all this sham knowledge and all
that supported it, and to lay an entirely new and clear
foundation to build on for the future; his assurance that,
as it was easy to point out with fatal and luminous
certainty the rottenness and hollowness of all existing
knowledge and philosophy, so it was equally easy to
devise and practically apply new and natural methods
of investigation and construction, which should replace
it by knowledge of infallible truth and boundless fruit-
fulness. His object,—to gain the key to the interpretation of nature; his method,—to gain it, not by the

means common to all previous schools of philosophy, by
untested reasonings and imposing and high-sounding
generalisations, but by a series and scale of rigorously
verified inductions, starting from the lowest facts of experience to discoveries which should prove and realise
themselves by leading deductively to practical results
—these, in one form or another, were the theme of his
philosophical writings from the earliest sight of them
that we gain.

He had disclosed what was in his mind in the letter
to Lord Burghley, written when he was thirty-one
($15\frac{90}{91}$), in which he announced that he had "taken all
knowledge for his province," to "purge it of 'frivolous
disputations' and 'blind experiments,' and that whatever happened to him, he meant to be a 'true pioner
in the mine of truth.'" But the first public step in the
opening of his great design was the publication in the
autumn of 1605 of the *Advancement of Learning*, a careful and balanced report on the existing stock and de-
ficiences of human knowledge. His endeavours, as he
says in the *Advancement* itself, are "but as an image in
a cross-way, that may point out the way, but cannot go
it." But from this image of his purpose, his thoughts
greatly widened, as time went on. The *Advancement*,
in part at least, was probably a hurried work. It
shadowed out, but only shadowed out, the lines of his
proposed reform of philosophical thought; it showed
his dissatisfaction with much that was held to be sound
and complete, and showed the direction of his ideas and
hopes. But it was many years before he took a further
step. Active life intervened. In 1620, at the height
of his prosperity, on the eve of his fall, he published

the long meditated *Novum Organum*, the avowed challenge to the old philosophies, the engine and instrument
of thought and discovery which was to put to shame
and supersede all others, containing, in part at least, the
principles of that new method of the use of experience
which was to be the key to the interpretation and
command of nature, and, together with the method, an
elaborate but incomplete exemplification of its leading
processes. Here were summed up, and stated with the
most solemn earnestness, the conclusions to which long
study and continual familiarity with the matters in
question had led him. And with the *Novum Organum*
was at length disclosed, though only in outline, the
whole of the vast scheme in all its parts, object, method,
materials, results, for the "Instauration" of human
knowledge, the restoration of powers lost, disused, neglected, latent, but recoverable by honesty, patience,
courage, and industry.

The *Instauratio*, as he planned the work, "is to be divided,"
says Mr. Ellis, "into six portions, of which the *first* is to contain
a general survey of the present state of knowledge. In the *second*,
men are to be taught how to use their understanding aright in the
investigation of nature. In the *third*, all the phenomena of the
universe are to be stored up as in a treasure-house, as the materials
on which the new method is to be employed. In the *fourth*, examples are to be given of its operation and of the results to which
it leads. The *fifth* is to contain what Bacon had accomplished in
natural philosophy *without* the aid of his own method ; *ex eodem
intellectûs usu quem alii in inquirendo et inveniendo adhibere con-
sueverunt.* It is therefore less important than the rest, and Bacon
declares that he will not bind himself to the conclusions which it
contains. Moreover, its value will altogether cease when the *sixth*
part can be completed, wherein will be set forth the new philosophy
—the results of the application of the new method to all the

phenomena of the universe. But to complete this, the last part of the *Instauratio*, Bacon does not hope ; he speaks of it as a thing, *et supra vires et ultra spes nostras collocata."—Works*, i. 71.

The *Novum Organum*, itself imperfect, was the crown of all that he lived to do. It was followed (1622) by the publication, intended to be periodical, of materials for the new philosophy to work upon, particular sections and classes of observations on phenomena—the *History of the Winds*, the *History of Life and Death*. Others were partly prepared but not published by him. And finally, in 1623, he brought out in Latin a greatly enlarged recasting of the *Advancement ;* the nine books of the *"De Augmentis."* But the great scheme was not completed : portions were left more or less finished. Much that he purposed was left undone, and could not have been yet done at that time.

But the works which he published represent imperfectly the labour spent on the undertaking. Besides these, there remains a vast amount of unused or rejected work, which shows how it was thought out, rearranged, tried first in one fashion and then in another, recast, developed. Separate chapters, introductions, "experimental essays and discarded beginnings," treatises with picturesque and imaginative titles, succeeded one another in that busy workshop ; and these first draughts and tentative essays have in them some of the freshest and most felicitous forms of his thoughts. At one time his enterprise, connecting itself with his own life and mission, rose before his imagination and kindled his feelings, and embodied itself in the lofty and stately "Proem" already quoted. His quick and brilliant imagination saw shadows and figures of his ideas in the ancient mythology, which

he worked out with curious ingenuity and often much
poetry, in his *Wisdom of the Ancients*. Towards the end
of his life he began to embody his thoughts and plans in
a philosophical tale, which he did not finish, the *New
Atlantis*, a charming example of his graceful fancy and of
his power of easy and natural story-telling. Between the
Advancement and the *Novum Organum* (1605-20) much
underground work had been done. "He had finally
(about 1607) settled the plan of the *Great Instauration,*
and began to call it by that name." The plan, first in
three or four divisions, had been finally digested into
six. Vague outlines had become definite and clear.
Distinct portions had been worked out. Various modes
of treatment had been tried, abandoned, modified. Prefaces were written to give the sketch and purpose of
chapters not yet composed. The *Novum Organum* had
been written and rewritten twelve times over. Bacon
kept his papers, and we can trace in the unused portion
of those left behind him much of the progress of his
work, and the shapes which much of it went through.
The *Advancement* itself is the filling out and perfecting
of what is found in germ, meagre and rudimentary, in
a *Discourse in Praise of Knowledge*, written in the days
of Elizabeth, and in some Latin chapters of an early
date, the *Cogitationes de Scientia Humana*, on the
limits and use of knowledge, and on the relation of
natural history to natural philosophy. These early
essays, with much of the same characteristic illustration,
and many of the favourite images and maxims and texts
and phrases, which continue to appear in his writings
to the end, contain the thoughts of a man long accustomed to meditate and to see his way on the new

aspects of knowledge, opening upon him. And before
the *Advancement*, he had already tried his hand on a
work intended to be in two books, which Mr. Ellis
describes as a "great work on the Interpretation of
Nature," the "earliest type of the *Instauratio*," and
which Bacon called by the enigmatical name of *Valerius
Terminus*. In it, as in a second draft, which in its turn
was superseded by the *Advancement*, the line of thought
of the Latin *Cogitationes* reappears, expanded and more
carefully ordered ; it contains also the first sketch of his
certain and infallible method for what he calls the
"freeing of the direction" in the search after Truth, and
the first indications of the four classes of "Idols"
which were to be so memorable a portion of Bacon's
teaching. And between the *Advancement* and the *Novum
Organum* at least one unpublished treatise of great
interest intervened, the *Visa et Cogitata*, on which he
was long employed, and which he brought to a finished
shape, fit to be submitted to his friends and critics, Sir
Thomas Bodley and Bishop Andrewes. It is spoken of
as a book to be "imparted *sicut videbitur*," in the review
which he made of his life and objects soon after he was
made Solicitor in 1608. A number of fragments also
bear witness to the fierce scorn and wrath which
possessed him against the older and the received philosophies. He tried his hand at declamatory onslaughts
on the leaders of human wisdom from the early Greeks
and Aristotle down to the latest "novellists ;" and he
certainly succeeded in being magnificently abusive.
But he thought wisely that this was not the best way
of doing what in the *Commentarius Solutus* he calls on
himself to do — "taking a greater confidence and

authority in discourses of this nature, *tanquam sui
certus et de alto despiciens;* " and the rhetorical *Redargutio
Philosophiarum*, and writings of kindred nature were
laid aside by his more serious judgment. But all
these fragments witness to the immense and unwearied
labour bestowed in the midst of a busy life on his undertaking; they suggest, too, the suspicion that there was
much waste from interruption, and the doubt whether
his work would not have been better if it could have
been more steadily continuous. But if ever a man had
a great object in life and pursued it through good and
evil report, through ardent hope and keen disappointment, to the end, with unwearied patience and un-
shaken faith, it was Bacon, when he sought the
improvement of human knowledge "for the glory of
God and the relief of man's estate." It is not the least
part of the pathetic fortune of his life that his own
success was so imperfect.

When a reader first comes, from the vague popular
notions of Bacon's work, to his definite proposals,
the effect is startling. Every one has heard that he
contemplated a complete reform of the existing conceptions of human knowledge, and of the methods by
which knowledge was to be sought; that rejecting them
as vitiated by the loose and untested way in which they
had been formed, he called men from verbal generalisations and unproved assumptions to come down face to
face with the realities of experience; that he substituted
for formal reasoning from baseless premisses and un-
meaning principles a methodical system of cautious and
sifting inference from wide observation and experiment;
and that he thus opened the path which modern science

thenceforth followed, with its amazing and unexhausted discoveries, and its vast and beneficent practical results. We credit all this to Bacon, and assuredly not without reason. All this is what was embraced in his vision of a changed world of thought and achievement. All this is what was meant by that *Regnum Hominis*, which, with a play on sacred words which his age did not shrink from, and which he especially pleased himself with, marked the coming of that hitherto unimagined empire of man over the powers and forces which encompassed him. But the detail of all this is multifarious and complicated, and is not always what we expect; and when we come to see how his work is estimated by those who, by greatest familiarity with scientific ideas and the history of scientific inquiries, are best fitted to judge of it, many a surprise awaits us.

For we find that the greatest differences of opinion exist on the value of what he did. Not only very unfavourable judgments have been passed upon it, on general grounds, as an irreligious, or a shallow and one-sided, or a poor and "utilitarian" philosophy, and on a definite comparison of it with the actual methods and processes which as a matter of history have been the real means of scientific discovery—but also some of those who have most admired his genius, and with the deepest love and reverence have spared no pains to do it full justice, have yet come to the conclusion that as an instrument and real method of work Bacon's attempt was a failure. It is not only De Maistre and Lord Macaulay who dispute his philosophical eminence. It is not only the depreciating opinion of a contemporary like Harvey, who was actually doing what

Bacon was writing about. It is not only that men who after the long history of modern science have won their place among its leaders, and are familiar by daily experience with the ways in which it works—a chemist like Liebig, a physiologist like Claude Bernard—say that they can find nothing to help them in Bacon's methods. It is not only that a clear and exact critic like M. de Rémusat looks at his attempt with its success and failure as characteristic of English massive practical good sense rather than as marked by real philosophical depth and refinement, such as Continental thinkers point to and are proud of in Descartes and Leibnitz. It is not even that a competent master of the whole domain of knowledge, Whewell, filled with the deepest sense of all that the world owes to Bacon, takes for granted that "though Bacon's general maxims are sagacious and animating, his particular precepts failed in his hands, and are now practically useless;" and assuming that Bacon's method is not the right one, and not complete as far as the progress of science up to his time could direct it, proceeds to construct a *Novum Organum Renovatum*. But Bacon's writings have recently undergone the closest examination by two editors, whose care for his memory is as loyal and affectionate as their capacity is undoubted, and their willingness to take trouble boundless. And Mr. Ellis and Mr. Spedding, with all their interest in every detail of Bacon's work, and admiration of the way in which he performed it, make no secret of their conclusion that he failed in the very thing on which he was most bent—the discovery of practical and fruitful ways of scientific inquiry. "Bacon," says Mr. Spedding, "failed to devise a practicable method for the discovery of the Forms of Nature because he misconceived the conditions of the case. . . . For the same reason he failed to make any single discovery which holds its place as one of the steps by which science has in any direction really advanced. The clue with which he entered the labyrinth did not reach far enough; before he had nearly attained his end he was obliged either to come back or to go on without it."

"His peculiar system of philosophy," says Mr. Spedding in another preface, "that is to say, the peculiar method of investigation, the "*organum*," the "*formula*," the "*clavis*," the "*ars ipsa interpretandi naturam*," the "*filum Labyrinthi*," or by whatever of its many names we choose to call that artificial process by which alone he believed man could attain a knowledge of the laws and a command over the powers of nature—*of this philosophy we can make nothing*. If we have not tried it, it is because we feel confident that it would not answer. We regard it as a curious piece of machinery, very subtle, elaborate, and ingenious, but not worth constructing, because all the work it could do may be done more easily another way."—*Works*, iii. 171.

What his method really was is itself a matter of question. Mr. Ellis speaks of it as a matter "but imperfectly apprehended." He differs from his fellow-labourer Mr. Spedding, in what he supposes to be its central and characteristic innovation. Mr. Ellis finds it in an improvement and perfection of logical machinery. Mr. Spedding finds it in the formation of a great "natural and experimental history," a vast collection of facts in every department of nature, which was to be a more important part of his philosophy than the *Novum Organum* itself. Both of them think that as he went on the difficulties of the work grew upon him, and caused alterations in his plans, and we are reminded that "there is no didactic exposi-

tion of his method in the whole of his writings," and
that " this has not been sufficiently remarked by those
who have spoken of his philosophy."

In the first place, the kind of intellectual instrument
which he proposed to construct was a mistake. His
great object was to place the human mind "on a level
with things and nature " (*ut faciamus intellectum humanum
rebus et naturæ parem*), and this could only be done by a
revolution in methods.   The ancients had all that genius
could do for man ; but it was a matter, he said, not of
the strength and fleetness of the running, but of the
rightness of the way.   It was a new method, absolutely different from anything known, which he proposed
to the world, and which should lead men to knowledge,
with the certainty and with the impartial facility of a
high road.   The Induction which he imagined to himself
as the contrast to all that had yet been tried was to have
two qualities.   It was to end, by no very prolonged or
difficult processes, in absolute certainty.   And next, it
was to leave very little to the differences of intellectual
power : it was to level minds and capacities.   It was to
give all men the same sort of power which a pair of
compasses gives the hand in drawing a circle.   "*Absolute
certainty, and a mechanical mode of procedure,*" says
Mr. Ellis, "*such that all men should be capable of em-
ploying it, are the two great features of the Baconian
system.*"   This he thought possible, and this he set
himself to expound—"a method universally applicable,
and in all cases infallible."   In this he saw the novelty
and the vast importance of his discovery.   "By this
method all the knowledge which the human mind was
capable of receiving might be attained, and attained

without unnecessary labour." It was a method of "a demonstrative character, with the power of reducing all minds to nearly the same level." The conception, indeed, of a "great Art of knowledge," of an "Instauration" of the sciences, of a "Clavis" which should unlock the difficulties which had hindered discovery—was not a new one. This attempt at a method, which should be certain, which should level capacities, which should do its work in a short time, had a special attraction for the imagination of the wild spirits of the South, from Raimond Lulli in the thirteenth century to the audacious Calabrians of the sixteenth. With Bacon it was something much more serious and reasonable and business-like. But such a claim has never yet been verified; there is no reason to think that it ever can be; and to have made it shows a fundamental defect in Bacon's conception of the possibilities of the human mind and the field it has to work in.

In the next place, though the prominence which he gave to the doctrine of Induction was one of those novelties which are so obvious after the event, though so strange before it, and was undoubtedly the element in his system which gave it life and power and influence on the course of human thought and discovery, his account of Induction was far from complete and satisfactory. Without troubling himself about the theory of Induction, as De Rémusat has pointed out, he contented himself with applying to its use the precepts of common-sense and a sagacious perception of the circumstances in which it was to be employed. But even these precepts, notable as they were, wanted distinctness and the qualities needed for working rules. The change is

great when in fifty years we pass from the poetical
science of Bacon to the mathematical and precise science
of Newton. His own time may well have been struck
by the originality and comprehensiveness of such a discriminating arrangement of proofs as the "Prerogative
Instances" of the *Novum Organum,* so natural and real,
yet never before thus compared and systematized. But
there is a great interval between his method of experi-
menting, his "*Hunt of Pan*"—the three tables of Instances, "*Presence,*" "*Absence,*" and "*Degrees, or Comparisons,*"
leading to a process of sifting and exclusion, and to the
First Vintage, or beginnings of theory — and say, for
instance, Mill's four methods of experimental inquiry,
the method of *agreement,* of *differences,* of *residues,* and
of *concomitant variations.* The course which he marked
out so laboriously and so ingeniously for Induction to
follow was one which was found to be impracticable, and
as barren of results as those deductive philosophies on
which he lavished his scorn. He has left precepts and
examples of what he meant by his cross-examining and
sifting processes. As admonitions to cross-examine and
to sift facts and phenomena they are valuable. Many
of the observations and classifications are subtle and in-
structive. But in his hands nothing comes of them.
They lead at the utmost to mere negative conclusions;
they show what a thing is not. But his attempt to elicit
anything positive out of them breaks down, or ends at
best in divinations and guesses, sometimes—as in connecting Heat and Motion—very near to later and more
carefully-grounded theories, but always unverified. He
had a radically false and mechanical conception, though
in words he earnestly disclaims it, of the way to deal

with the facts of nature. He looked on them as things
which told their own story, and suggested the questions
which ought to be put to them ; and with this idea half
his time was spent in collecting huge masses of indigested
facts of the most various authenticity and value, and he
thought he was collecting materials which his method
had only to touch in order to bring forth from them light
and truth and power. He thought that, not in certain
sciences, but in all, one set of men could do the observ-
ing and collecting, and another be set on the work of
Induction and the discovery of "axioms." Doubtless in
the arrangement and sorting of them his versatile and
ingenious mind gave itself full play ; he divides and distinguishes them into their companies and groups, different kinds of Motion, "Prerogative" instances with
their long tale of imaginative titles. But we look in
vain for any use that he was able to make of them,
or even to suggest. Bacon never adequately realised
that no promiscuous assemblage of even the most
certain facts could ever lead to knowledge, could ever
suggest their own interpretation, without the action on
them of the living mind, without the initiative of an idea.
In truth he was so afraid of assumptions and "anticipations" and prejudices—his great bugbear was so much
the "*intellectus sibi permissus*," the mind given liberty to
guess and imagine and theorise, instead of, as it ought,
absolutely and servilely submitting itself to the control
of facts, that he missed the true place of the rational and
formative element in his account of Induction. He does
tell us, indeed, that "truth emerges sooner from error
than from confusion." He indulges the mind, in the
course of its investigation of "Instances," with a first

O

"vintage" of provisional generalisations. But of the way in which the living mind of the discoverer works, with its ideas, and insight, and thoughts that come no one knows whence, working hand in hand with what comes before the eye or is tested by the instrument, he gives us no picture. Compare his elaborate investigation of the "Form of Heat" in the *Novum Organum* with such a record of real inquiry as Wells' *Treatise on Dew*, or Herschel's analysis of it in his *Introduction to Natural Philosophy*. And of the difference of genius between a Faraday or a Newton, and the crowd of average men who have used and finished off their work, he takes no account. Indeed, he thinks that for the future such difference is to disappear.

"That his method is impracticable," says Mr. Ellis, "cannot, I think, be denied, if we reflect not only that it never has produced any result, but also that the process by which scientific truths have been established cannot be so presented as even to appear to be in accordance with it. In all cases this process involves an element to which nothing corresponds in the Tables of 'Comparence' and 'Exclusion,' namely, the application to the facts of observation of a principle of arrangement, an idea, existing in the mind of the discoverer antecedently to the act of induction. It may be said that this idea is precisely one of the *naturæ* into which the facts of observation ought in Bacon's system to be analysed. And this is in one sense true; but it must be added that this analysis, if it be thought right so to call it, is of the essence of the discovery which results from it. In most cases the act of induction follows as a matter of course as soon as the appropriate idea has been introduced."—(Ellis, *General Preface*, i. 38.)

Lastly, not only was Bacon's conception of philosophy so narrow as to exclude one of its greatest domains; for, says Mr. Ellis, "it cannot be denied that to Bacon all sound philosophy seemed to be included in what we now

call the natural sciences," and in all its parts was claimed
as the subject of his inductive method; but Bacon's
scientific knowledge and scientific conceptions were often
very imperfect—more imperfect than they ought to have
been for his time. Of one large part of science, which
was just then beginning to be cultivated with high
promise of success, the knowledge of the heavens, he
speaks with a coldness and suspicion which contrasts
remarkably with his eagerness about things belonging to
the sphere of the earth, and within reach of the senses.
He holds, of course, the unity of the world ; the laws of
the whole visible universe are one order; but the heavens,
wonderful as they are to him, are—compared with other
things—out of his track of inquiry.   He had his astronomical theories ; he expounded them in his " *Descriptio
Globi Intellectualis* " and his *Thema Cœli*.   He was not
altogether ignorant of what was going on in days when
Copernicus, Kepler, and Galileo were at work.   But he
did not know how to deal with it, and there were men
in England, before and then, who understood much better
than he the problems and the methods of astronomy.
He had one conspicuous and strange defect for a man
who undertook what he did.   He was not a mathema-
tician : he did not see the indispensable necessity of
mathematics in the great *Instauration* which he projected ;
he did not much believe in what they could do.   He
cared so little about them that he takes no notice of
Napier's invention of Logarithms.   He was not able to
trace how the direct information of the senses might be
rightly subordinated to the rational, but not self-evident
results of geometry and arithmetic.   He was impatient
of the subtleties of astronomical calculations ; they only

attempted to satisfy problems about the motion of bodies
in the sky, and told us nothing of physical fact : they
gave us, as Prometheus gave to Jove, the outside skin
of the offering, which was stuffed inside with straw and
rubbish.   He entirely failed to see that before dealing
with physical astronomy, it must be dealt with mathe-
matically.   "It is well to ·remark," as Mr. Ellis says,
"that none of Newton's astronomical discoveries could
have been made if astronomers had not continued to
render themselves liable to Bacon's censure."   Bacon
little thought that in navigation the compass itself
would become a subordinate instrument compared with
the helps given by mathematical astronomy.   In this,
and in other ways, Bacon rose above his time in his conceptions of what *might be*, but not of what *was;* the list
is a long one, as given by Mr. Spedding (iii. 511), of the
instances which show that he was ill-informed about
the advances of knowledge in his own time.   And his
mind was often not clear when he came to deal with
complex phenomena.   Thus, though he constructed a
table of specific gravities—"the only collection," says
Mr. Ellis, " of quantitative experiments that we find in
his works," and "wonderfully accurate considering the
manner in which they were obtained ; " yet he failed to
understand the real nature of the famous experiment of
Archimedes.   And so with the larger features of his
teaching it is impossible not to feel how imperfectly he
had emancipated himself from the power of words, and
of common prepossessions ; how for one reason or
another he had failed to call himself to account in the
terms he employed, and the assumptions on which he
argued.   The caution does not seem to have occurred to

him that the statement of a fact may, in nine cases out
of ten, involve a theory. His whole doctrine of "Forms,"
and "Simple natures," which is so prominent in his method
of investigation, is an example of loose and slovenly
use of unexamined and untested ideas. He allowed
himself to think that it would be possible to arrive at
an alphabet of nature, which, once attained, would suffice
to spell out and constitute all its infinite combinations.
He accepted, without thinking it worth a doubt, the
doctrine of appetites, and passions, and inclinations, and
dislikes, and horrors, in inorganic nature.   His whole
physiology of life and death depends on a doctrine of
animal spirits, of which he traces the operations and
qualities as if they were as certain as the nerves or the
blood, and of which he gives this account—" that in
every tangible body there is a spirit covered and
enveloped in the grosser body;" "not a virtue, not an
energy, not an actuality, nor any such idle matter, but
a body thin and invisible, and yet having place, and
dimension, and real." . . . "a middle nature between
flame, which is momentary, and air which is permanent."
Yet these are the very things for which he holds up
Aristotle and the Scholastics and the Italian speculators
to reprobation and scorn.   The clearness of his thinking
was often overlaid by the immense profusion of decor-
ative material which his meditation brought along with
it.   The defect was greater than that which even his
ablest defenders admit.   It was more than that in that
"greatest and radical difference, which he himself observes" between minds, the difference between minds
which were apt to note *distinctions*, and those which were
apt to note *likenesses*, he was, without knowing it, defec-

tive in the first. It was that in many instances, he exemplified in his own work the very faults which he charged on the older philosophies : haste, carelessness, precipitancy, using words without thinking them out, assuming to know when he ought to have perceived his real ignorance.

What then, with all these mistakes and failures, not always creditable or pardonable, has given Bacon his pre-eminent place in the history of science ?

1. The answer is that with all his mistakes and failures, the principles on which his mode of attaining a knowledge of nature was based were the only true ones ; and they had never before been propounded so systematically, so fully, and so earnestly. His was not the first mind on whom these principles had broken. Men were, and had been for some time, pursuing their inquiries into various departments of nature precisely on the general plan of careful and honest observation of real things which he enjoined. They had seen, as he saw, the futility of all attempts at natural philosophy by mere thinking and arguing, without coming into contact with the contradictions, or corrections, or verifications of experience. In Italy, in Germany, in England there were laborious and successful workers, who had long felt that to be in touch with nature was the only way to know. But no one had yet come before the world to proclaim this on the house-tops, as the key of the only certain path to the secrets of nature, the watchword of a revolution in the methods of interpreting her ; and this Bacon did with an imposing authority and power which enforced attention. He spoke the thoughts of patient toilers like Harvey with a largeness and richness which they could

not command, and which they perhaps smiled at.   He
disentangled and spoke the vague thoughts of his age,
which other men had not the courage and clearness of
mind to formulate.   What Bacon *did*, indeed, and what
he *meant*, are separate matters.   He *meant* an infallible
method by which man should be fully equipped for a
struggle with nature : he meant an irresistible and immediate conquest, within a definite and not distant time.
It was too much.   He himself saw no more of what he
meant than Columbus did of America.   But what he *did*
was, to persuade men for the future that the intelligent,
patient, persevering cross-examination of things, and the
thoughts about them, was the only, and was the successful road to know.   No one had yet done this, and he
did it.   His writings were a public recognition of real
science, in its humblest tasks about the commonplace
facts before our feet, as well as in its loftiest achievements.   " The man who is growing great and happy by
electrifying a bottle," says Dr. Johnson, " wonders to
see the world engaged in the prattle about peace and
war," and the world was ready to smile at the simplicity
or the impertinence of his enthusiasm.   Bacon impressed
upon the world for good, with every resource of subtle
observation and forcible statement, that " the man who
is growing great by electrifying a bottle," is as important
a person in the world's affairs as the arbiter of peace and
war.

2. Yet this is not all.   An inferior man might have
made himself the mouthpiece of the hopes and aspirations of his generation after a larger science.   But to
Bacon these aspirations embodied themselves in the form
of a great and absorbing idea; an idea which took pos-

session of the whole man, kindling in him a faith which
nothing could quench, and a passion which nothing could
dull; an idea which, for forty years, was his daily companion, his daily delight, his daily business; an idea
which he was never tired of placing in ever fresh and
more attractive lights, from which no trouble could
wean him, about which no disaster could make him
despair; an idea round which the instincts and intui-
tions and obstinate convictions of genius gathered, which
kindled his rich imagination, and was invested by it with
a splendour and magnificence like the dreams of fable.
It is this idea which finds its fitting expression in the
grand and stately aphorisms of the *Novum Organum*, in
the varied fields of interest in the *De Augmentis*, in
the romance of the *New Atlantis*. It is this idea, this
certainty of a new unexplored Kingdom of Knowledge
within the reach and grasp of man, if he will be humble
enough, and patient enough, and truthful enough to
occupy it—this announcement not only of a new system
of thought, but of a change in the condition of the world,
a prize and possession such as man had not yet imagined,
this belief in the fortunes of the human race and its issue,
"such an issue, it may be, as in the present condition of
things and men's minds cannot easily be conceived or
imagined," yet more than verified in the wonders which
our eyes have seen—it is this which gives its prerogative
to Bacon's work. That he bungled about the processes
of Induction, that he talked about an unintelligible doctrine of *Forms*, did not affect the weight and solemnity
of his call to learn, so full of wisdom and good sense, so
sober and so solid, yet so audaciously confident. There
had been nothing like it in its ardour of hope, in the

glory which it threw around the investigation of nature.
It was the presence and the power of a great idea—long
become a commonplace to us, but strange and perplexing
at first to his own generation, which probably shared
Coke's opinion that it qualified its champion for a place
in the company of the "Ship of Fools," which expressed
its opinion of the man who wrote the *Novum Organum*
in the sentiment that "a fool *could* not have written it,
and a wise man *would* not "—it is this which has placed
Bacon among the great discoverers of the human race.

It is this imaginative yet serious assertion of the vast
range and possibilities of human knowledge which, as M.
de Rémusat remarks, the keenest and fairest of Bacon's
judges, gives Bacon his claim to the undefinable but very
real character of greatness.   Two men stand out, "the
masters of those who know," without equals up to their
time, among men—the Greek Aristotle and the Englishman Bacon.   They agree in the universality and comprehensiveness of their conception of human knowledge ;
and they were absolutely alone in their serious practical
ambition to work out this conception.   In the separate
departments of thought, of investigation, of art, each is
left far behind by numbers of men, who in these separate
departments have gone far deeper than they, have soared
higher, have been more successful in what they attempted.
But Aristotle first, and for his time more successfully,
and Bacon after him, ventured on the daring enterprise
of "taking all knowledge for their province ;" and in
this they stood alone.   This present scene of man's
existence, this that we call nature, the stage on which
mortal life begins and goes on and ends, the faculties
with which man is equipped to act, to enjoy, to create,

to hold his way amid or against the circumstances and forces round him—this is what each wants to know, as thoroughly and really as can be. It is not to reduce things to a theory or a system that they look around them on the place where they find themselves with life and thought and power: that were easily done, and has been done over and over again, only to prove its futility. It is to know, as to the whole and its parts, as men understand *knowing* in some one subject of successful handling, whether art, or science, or practical craft. This idea, this effort, distinguishes these two men. The Greeks—predecessors, contemporaries, successors of Aristotle—were speculators, full of clever and ingenious guesses, in which the amount of clear and certain fact was in lamentable disproportion to the schemes blown up from it; or they devoted themselves more profitably to some one or two subjects of inquiry, moral or purely intellectual, with absolute indifference to what might be asked, or what might be known, of the real conditions under which they were passing their existence. Some of the Romans, Cicero and Pliny, had encyclopædic minds; but the Roman mind was the slave of precedent, and was more than satisfied with partially understanding and neatly arranging what the Greeks had left. The Arabians looked more widely about them ; but the Arabians were essentially sceptics, and resigned subjects to the inevitable and the inexplicable ; there was an irony, open or covert, in their philosophy, their termino-logy, their transcendental mysticism, which showed how little they believed that they really knew. The vast and mighty intellects of the schoolmen never came into a real grapple with the immensity of the facts of the

natural or even of the moral world; within the world
of abstract thought, the world of language with its infinite growths and consequences, they have never had
their match for keenness, for patience, for courage, for
inexhaustible toil; but they were as much disconnected
from the natural world, which was their stage of life, as
if they had been disembodied spirits. The Renaissance
brought with it not only the desire to know, but to
know comprehensively and in all possible directions; it
brought with it temptations to the awakened Italian
genius, renewed, enlarged, refined, if not strengthened
by its passage through the Middle Ages, to make thought
deal with the real, and to understand the scene in which
men were doing such strange and wonderful things; but
Giordano Bruno, Telesio, Campanella, and their fellows,
were not men capable of more than short flights, though
they might be daring and eager ones. It required more
thoroughness, more humble-minded industry, to match
the magnitude of the task. And there have been men
of universal minds and comprehensive knowledge since
Bacon, Leibnitz, Goethe, Humboldt, men whose thoughts
were at home everywhere, where there was something
to be known. But even for them the world of knowledge has grown too large. We shall never again see
an Aristotle or a Bacon, because the conditions of knowledge have altered. Bacon, like Aristotle, belonged to
an age of adventure, which went to sea little knowing
whither it went, and ill furnished with knowledge and
instruments. He entered with a vast and vague scheme
of discovery on these unknown seas and new worlds,
which to us are familiar and daily traversed in every
direction. This new world of knowledge has turned out

in many ways very different from what Aristotle or
Bacon supposed, and has been conquered by implements
and weapons very different in precision and power from
what they purposed to rely on.   But the combination of
patient and careful industry, with the courage and
divination of genius, in doing what none had done
before, makes it equally stupid and idle to impeach their
greatness.

3. Bacon has been charged with bringing philosophy
down from the heights, not as of old to make men know
themselves, and to be the teacher of the highest form
of truth, but to be the purveyor of material utility.   It
contemplates only, it is said, the "*commoda vitæ;*" about
the deeper and more elevating problems of thought it
does not trouble itself.   It concerns itself only about
external and sensible nature, about what is "of the
earth, earthy."   But when it comes to the questions
which have attracted the keenest and hardiest thinkers,
the question, what it is that thinks and wills,—what is
the origin and guarantee of the faculties by which men
know anything at all and form rational and true conceptions about nature and themselves, whence it is that
reason draws its powers and materials and rules —
what is the meaning of words which all use but few
can explain—Time and Space, and Being and Cause, and
consciousness and choice, and the moral law—Bacon is
content with a loose and superficial treatment of them.
Bacon certainly was not a metaphysician, nor an exact
and lucid reasoner.   With wonderful flashes of sure intuition or happy anticipation, his mind was deficient in
the powers which deal with the deeper problems of
thought, just as it was deficient in the mathematical

faculty.   The subtlety, the intuition, the penetration,
the severe precision, even the force of imagination, which
make a man a great thinker on any abstract subject
were not his; the interest of questions which had interested metaphysicians had no interest for him: he
distrusted and undervalued them.   When he touches the
"ultimities" of knowledge he is as obscure and hard to
be understood as any of those restless Southern Italians
of his own age, who shared with him the ambition of
reconstructing science.   Certainly the science which
most interested Bacon, the science which he found as he
thought in so desperate a condition, and to which he
gave so great an impulse, was physical science.   But
physical science may be looked at and pursued in different ways, in different tempers, with different objects.
It may be followed in the spirit of Newton, of Boyle, of
Herschel, of Faraday ; or with a confined and low horizon it may be dwarfed and shrivelled into a mean utilitarianism.   But Bacon's horizon was not a narrow one.
He believed in God, and immortality, and the Christian
creed and hope.   To him the restoration of the Reign
of Man was a noble enterprise, because man was so
great and belonged to so great an order of things,
because the things which he was bid to search into with
honesty and truthfulness were the works and laws of
God, because it was so shameful and so miserable that
from an ignorance which industry and good sense could
remedy, the tribes of mankind passed their days in self-
imposed darkness and helplessness.   It was God's
appointment that men should go through this earthly
stage of their being.   Each stage of man's mysterious
existence had to be dealt with, not according to his own

fancies, but according to the conditions imposed on it ;
and it was one of man's first duties to arrange for his
stay on earth according to the real laws which he could
find out if he only sought for them. Doubtless it was
one of Bacon's highest hopes that from the growth of
true knowledge would follow in surprising ways the relief of man's estate ; this, as an end, runs through all
his yearning after a fuller and surer method of interpreting nature. The desire to be a great benefactor,
the spirit of sympathy and pity for mankind, reign
through this portion of his work—pity for confidence so
greatly abused by the teachers of man, pity for ignorance which might be dispelled, pity for pain and misery
which might be relieved.   In the quaint but beautiful
picture of courtesy, kindness, and wisdom, which he
imagines in the *New Atlantis*, the representative of true
philosophy, the " Father of Solomon's House," is introduced as one who "had an aspect as if he pitied men."
But unless it is utilitarianism to be keenly alive to the
needs and pains of life, and to be eager and busy to
lighten and assuage them, Bacon's philosophy was not
utilitarian. It may deserve many reproaches, but not
this one. Such a passage as the following—in which
are combined the highest motives and graces and passions
of the soul, love of truth, humility of mind, purity of
purpose, reverence for God, sympathy for man, compas-
sion for the sorrows of the world and longing to heal
them, depth of conviction and faith—fairly represents
the spirit which runs through his works. After urging
the mistaken use of imagination and authority in science,
he goes on :—

    " There is not and never will be an end or limit to this ; one

catches at one thing, another at another ; each has his favourite
fancy ; pure and open light there is none ; every one philosophises
out of the cells of his own imagination, as out of Plato's cave ; the
higher wits with more acuteness and felicity, the duller, less happily
but with equal pertinacity.   And now of late by the regulation of
some learned and (as things now are) excellent men (the former
licence having, I suppose, become wearisome), the sciences are confined to certain and prescribed authors, and thus restrained are
imposed upon the old and instilled into the young ; so that now (to
use the sarcasm of Cicero concerning Cæsar's year), the constellation
of Lyra rises by edict, and authority is taken for truth, not truth
for authority.   Which kind of institution and discipline is excellent
for present use, but precludes all prospect of improvement.   For we
copy the sin of our first parents while we suffer for it.   They wished
to be like God, but their posterity wish to be even greater.   For
we create worlds, we direct and domineer over nature, we will have
it that all things *are* as in our folly we think they should be, not
as seems fittest to the Divine wisdom, or as they are found to be in
fact ; and I know not whether we more distort the facts of nature
or of our own wits ; but we clearly impress the stamp of our own
image on the creatures and works of God, instead of carefully examining and recognising in them the stamp of the Creator himself.
Wherefore our dominion over creatures is a second time forfeited,
not undeservedly ; and whereas after the fall of man some power
over the resistance of creatures was still left to him—the power of
subduing and managing them by true and solid arts—yet this too
through our insolence, and because we desire to be like God and to
follow the dictates of our own reason, we in great part lose.   If,
therefore, there be any humility towards the Creator, any reverence
for or disposition to magnify His works, any charity for man and
anxiety to relieve his sorrows and necessities, any love of truth in
nature, any hatred of darkness, any desire for the purification of
the understanding, we must entreat men again and again to discard,
or at least set apart for a while, these volatile and preposterous
philosophies which have preferred theses to hypotheses, led experience captive, and triumphed over the works of God ; and to approach with humility and veneration to unroll the volume of
Creation, to linger and meditate therein, and with minds washed
clean from opinions to study it in purity and integrity.   For this

is that sound and language which "went forth into all lands," and
did not incur the confusion of Babel; this should men study to be
perfect in, and becoming again as little children condescend to take
the alphabet of it into their hands, and spare no pains to search
and unravel the interpretation thereof, but pursue it strenuously
and persevere even unto death."—(Preface to *Historia Naturalis:*
translated, *Works*, v. 132-3.)

CHAPTER IX.

BACON AS A WRITER.

BACON'S name belongs to letters as well as to philosophy. In his own day, whatever his contemporaries thought of his *Instauration of Knowledge*, he was in the first rank as a speaker and a writer. Sir Walter Raleigh, contrasting him with Salisbury, who could speak but not write, and Northampton, who could write but not speak, thought Bacon eminent both as a speaker and a writer. Ben Jonson, passing in review the more famous names of his own and the preceding age, from Sir Thomas More to Sir Philip Sidney, Hooker, Essex and Raleigh, places Bacon without a rival at the head of the company as the man who had "fulfilled all numbers," and "stood as the mark and ἀκμὴ of our language." And he also records Bacon's power as a speaker. "No man," he says, "ever spoke more neatly, more pressly, or suffered less emptiness, less idleness, in what he uttered." . . . "His hearers could not cough or look aside from him without loss. He commanded when he spoke, and had his judges angry and pleased at his devotion . . . the fear of every man that heard him was that he should make an end." He notices one feature for which we are less prepared, though we know that

P

the edge of Bacon's sarcastic tongue was felt and resented
in James's Court. "His speech," says Ben Jonson,
"was nobly censorious when he could *spare and pass by
a jest.*" The unpopularity which certainly seems to
have gathered round his name may have had something
to do with this reputation.

Yet as an English writer Bacon did not expect to be
remembered, and he hardly cared to be. He wrote
much in Latin, and his first care was to have his books
put into a Latin dress. "For these modern languages,"
he wrote to Toby Matthew towards the close of his life,
"will at one time or another play the bank-rowte with
books, and since I have lost much time with this age, I
would be glad if God would give me leave to recover it
with posterity." He wanted to be read by the learned
out of England, who were supposed to appreciate his
philosophical ideas better than his own countrymen, and
the only way to this was to have his books translated
into the "general language." He sends Prince Charles
the *Advancement* in its new Latin dress. "It is a book,"
he says, "that will live, and be a citizen of the world,
as English books are not." And he fitted it for continental reading by carefully weeding it of all passages
that might give offence to the censors at Rome or Paris.
"I have been," he writes to the King, "mine own *Index
Expurgatorius*, that it may be read in all places. For
since my end of putting it in Latin was to have it read
everywhere, it had been an absurd contradiction to free
it in the language and to pen it up in the matter."
Even the *Essays* and the *History of Henry VII.* he had
put into Latin "by some good pens that do not forsake
me." Among these translators are said to have been

George Herbert and Hobbes, and on more doubtful
authority, Ben Jonson and Selden. The *Essays* were
also translated into Latin and Italian with Bacon's
sanction.

Bacon's contemptuous and hopeless estimate of "these
modern languages," forty years after Spenser had pro-
claimed and justified his faith in his own language, is
only one of the proofs of the short-sightedness of the
wisest and the limitations of the largest-minded. Perhaps we ought not to wonder at his silence about
Shakespeare. It was the fashion, except among a set
of clever but not always very reputable people, to think
the stage, as it was, below the notice of scholars and
statesmen; and Shakespeare took no trouble to save his
works from neglect. Yet it is a curious defect in Bacon
that he should not have been more alive to the powers
and future of his own language. He early and all along
was profoundly impressed with the contrast, which the
scholarship of the age so abundantly presented, of words
to things. He dwells in the *Advancement* on that "first
distemper of learning, when men study words and not
matter." He illustrates it at large from the reaction of
the new learning and of the popular teaching of the
Reformation against the utilitarian and unclassical
terminology of the schoolmen; a reaction which soon
grew to excess and made men "hunt more after choice-
ness of the phrase, and the round and clean composition
of the sentence and the sweet falling of the clauses,"
than after worth of subject, soundness of argument, "life
of invention or depth of judgment." "I have represented this," he says, "in an example of late times, but
it hath been and will be *secundum majus et minus* in all

times;" and he likens this "vanity" to "Pygmalion's
frenzy,"—"for to fall in love with words which are but
the images of matter, is all one as to fall in love with a
picture." He was dissatisfied with the first attempt at
translation into Latin of the *Advancement* by Dr.
Playfer of Cambridge, because he "desired not so much
neat and polite, as clear, masculine, and apt expression."
Yet, with this hatred of circumlocution and prettiness,
of the cloudy amplifications, and pompous flourishings,
and "the flowing and watery vein," which the scholars
of his time affected, it is strange that he should not have
seen that the new ideas and widening thoughts of which
he was the herald would want a much more elastic and
more freely-working instrument than Latin could ever
become. It is wonderful indeed what can be done with
Latin. It was long after his day to be the language of the
exact sciences. In his *History of the Winds*, which is full
of his irrepressible fancy and picturesqueness, Bacon
describes in clear and intelligible Latin the details of the
rigging of a modern man-of-war, and the mode of sailing
her. But such tasks impose a yoke, sometimes a rough
one, on a language which has "taken its ply" in very
different conditions, and of which the genius is that of
indirect and circuitous expression, "full of majesty and
circumstance." But it never, even in those days of scholarship, could lend itself to the frankness, the straight-
forwardness, the fullness and shades of suggestion and
association, with which, in handling ideas of subtlety and
difficulty, a writer would wish to speak to his reader, and
which he could find only in his mother tongue. It might
have been thought that with Bacon's contempt of form and
ceremony in these matters, his consciousness of the powers

of English in his hands might have led him to anticipate
that a flexible, and rich, and strong language might
create a literature, and that a literature, if worth studying, would be studied in its own language. But so great
a change was beyond even his daring thoughts. To him,
as to his age, the only safe language was the Latin. For
familiar use English was well enough. But it could not
be trusted; "it would play the bankrupt with books."
And yet Galileo was writing in Italian as well as in
Latin; only within twenty-five years later, Descartes
was writing *De la Méthode*, and Pascal was writing in
the same French in which he wrote the *Provincial Letters,*
his *Nouvelles Expériences touchant le Vide*, and the con-
troversial pamphlets which followed it; showing how
in that interval of five-and-twenty years an instrument
had been fashioned out of a modern language such as for
lucid expression and clear reasoning, Bacon had not yet
dreamed of. From Bacon to Pascal is the change from
the old scientific way of writing to the modern; from a
modern language as learned and used in the 16th century,
to one learned in the 17th.

But the language of the age of Elizabeth was a rich
and noble one, and it reached a high point in the hands
of Bacon. In his hands it lent itself to many uses, and
assumed many forms, and he valued it, not because he
thought highly of its qualities as a language, but
because it enabled him with least trouble "to speak
as he would," in throwing off the abundant thoughts
that rose within his mind, and in going through the
variety of business which could not be done in Latin.
But in all his writing it is the matter, the real thing that
he wanted to say, which was uppermost. He cared how

it was said, not for the sake of form or ornament, but
because the force and clearness of what was said depended
so much on how it was said. Of course, what he wanted
to say varied indefinitely with the various occasions of
his life. His business may merely be to write "a device"
or panegyric for a pageant in the Queen's honour, or for
the revels of Gray's Inn. But even these trifles are
the result of real thought, and are full of ideas, ideas
about the hopes of knowledge or about the policy of
the State; and though, of course, they have plenty of the
flourishes and quaint absurdities indispensable on such
occasions, yet the "rhetorical affectation" is in the thing
itself, and not in the way it is handled : he had an
opportunity of saying some of the things which were to
him of deep and perpetual interest, and he used it to
say them, as forcibly, as strikingly, as attractively as he
could. His manner of writing depends, not on a style,
or a studied or acquired habit but on the nature of the
task which he has in hand. Everywhere his matter is
close to his words, and governs, animates, informs his
words. No one in England before had so much as he
had the power to say what he wanted to say, and
exactly as he wanted to say it. No one was so little at
the mercy of conventional language or customary rhetoric,
except when he persuaded himself that he had to submit
to those necessities of flattery, which cost him at last so
dear.

The book by which English readers, from his own time
to ours, have known him best, better than by the originality and the eloquence of the *Advancement*, or than by
the political weight and historical imagination of the
History of Henry VII., is the first book which he published,

the volume of *Essays*. It is an instance of his self-
willed but most skilful use of the freedom and ease
which the "modern language," which he despised, gave
him. It is obvious that he might have expanded these
"Counsels, moral and political," to the size which such
essays used to swell to after his time. Many people
would have thanked him for doing so ; and some have
thought it a good book on which to hang their own
reflections and illustrations. But he saw how much could
be done by leaving the beaten track of set treatise and
discourse, and setting down unceremoniously the observations which he had made and the real rules which he
had felt to be true, on various practical matters which
come home to men's "business and bosoms." He was
very fond of these moral and political generalisations,
both of his own collecting and as found in writers
who, he thought, had the right to make them, like
the Latins of the Empire and the Italians and Span-
iards of the Renaissance. But a mere string of
maxims and quotations would have been a poor thing
and not new ; and he cast what he had to say into
connected wholes. But nothing can be more loose than
the structure of the essays. There is no art, no style,
almost, except in a few, the political ones, no order :
thoughts are put down and left unsupported, unproved,
undeveloped. In the first form of the ten, which composed the first edition of 1597, they are more like notes
of analysis or tables of contents ; they are austere even
to meagreness. But the general character continues in
the enlarged and expanded ones of Bacon's later years.
They are like chapters in Aristotle's Ethics and Rhetoric
on virtues and characters ; only Bacon's takes Aristotle's

broad marking lines as drawn, and proceeds with the
subtler and more refined observations of a much longer and
wider experience.   But these short papers say what they
have to say without preface, and in literary undress, without a superfluous word, without the joints and bands of
structure: they say it in brief, rapid sentences, which come
down, sentence after sentence, like the strokes of a great
hammer.   No wonder that in their disdainful brevity they
seem rugged and abrupt, "and do not seem to end, but
fall."   But with their truth and piercingness and delicacy
of observation, their roughness gives a kind of flavour
which no elaboration could give.   It is none the less that
their wisdom is of a somewhat cynical kind, fully alive
to the slipperiness and self-deceits and faithlessness which
are in the world and rather inclined to be amused at
them.   In some we can see distinct records of the
writer's own experience : one contains the substance of a
charge delivered to Judge Hutton on his appointment;
another of them is a sketch drawn from life of a character
which had crossed Bacon's path, and in the essay on
Seeming Wise we can trace from the impatient notes
put down in his *Commentarius Solutus,* the picture of
the man who stood in his way, the Attorney-General
Hobart.   Some of them are memorable oracular utter-
ances not inadequate to the subject, on *Truth,* or *Death,*
or *Unity.*   Others reveal an utter incapacity to come near
a subject, except as a strange external phenomena, like the
essay on *Love.*   There is a distinct tendency in them to
the Italian school of political and moral wisdom, the
wisdom of distrust and of reliance on indirect and
roundabout ways.   There is a group of them, "of *Delays,*"
" of *Cunning,*" " of *Wisdom for a Man's Self,*" " of *Des-*

patch," which show how vigilantly and to what purpose
he had watched the treasurers and secretaries and
intriguers of Elizabeth's and James's Courts; and there
are curious self-revelations, as in the essay on *Friendship.*
But there are also currents of better and larger feeling,
such as those which show his own ideal of "*Great Place,*"
and what he felt of its dangers and duties. And mixed
with the fantastic taste and conceits of the time, there
is evidence in them of Bacon's keen delight in nature,
in the beauty and scents of flowers, in the charm of open
air life, as in the essay on *Gardens,* "The purest of
human pleasures, the greatest refreshment to the spirits
of man."

But he had another manner of writing for what he
held to be his more serious work. In the philosophical
and historical works there is no want of attention to the
flow and order and ornament of composition. When
we come to the *Advancement of Learning,* we come to a
book which is one of the landmarks of what high thought
and rich imagination have made of the English language.
It is the first great book in English prose of secular interest; the first book which can claim a place beside the
Laws of Ecclesiastical Polity. As regards its subject-
matter, it has been partly thrown into the shade by the
greatly enlarged and elaborate form in which it ulti-
mately appeared, in a Latin dress, as the first portion
of the scheme of the *Instauratio,* the *De Augmentis
Scientiarum.* Bacon looked on it as a first effort, a kind
of call-bell to awaken and attract the interest of others
in the thoughts and hopes which so interested himself.
But it contains some of his finest writing. In the *Essays*
he writes as a looker-on at the game of human affairs,

who, according to his frequent illustration, sees more of
it than the gamesters themselves, and is able to give
wiser and faithful counsel, not without a touch of kindly
irony at the mistakes which he observes.   In the
Advancement he is the enthusiast for a great cause and
a great hope, and all that he has of passion and power
is enlisted in the effort to advance it.   The *Advancement*
is far from being a perfect book.   As a survey of the
actual state of knowledge in his day, of its deficiencies
and what was wanted to supply them, it is not even
up to the materials of the time.   Even the improved
De Augmentis is inadequate ; and there is reason to
think the *Advancement* was a hurried book, at least in
the later part, and it is defective in arrangement and
proportion of parts.   Two of the great divisions of
knowledge — history and poetry — are despatched in
comparatively short chapters ; while in the division on
" Civil Knowledge," human knowledge as it respects
society, he inserts a long essay, obviously complete in
itself and clumsily thrust in here, on the ways of
getting on in the world, the means by which a man may
be " *Faber fortunæ suæ* "—the architect of his own success ;
too lively a picture to be pleasant of the arts with which
he had become acquainted in the process of rising.   The
book, too, has the blemishes of its own time ; its want
of simplicity, its inevitable though very often amusing
and curious pedantries.   But the *Advancement* was the
first of a long line of books which have attempted to
teach English readers how to think of knowledge ; to
make it really and intelligently the interest, not of the
school or the study or the laboratory only, but of society
at large.   It was a book with a purpose, new then, but

of which we have seen the fulfilment. He wanted to
impress on his generation, as a very practical matter, all
that knowledge might do in wise hands, all that knowledge had lost by the faults and errors of men and the
misfortunes of time, all that knowledge might be pushed
to in all directions by faithful and patient industry and
well-planned methods for the elevation and benefit of
man in his highest capacities as well as in his humblest.
And he further sought to teach them *how* to know; to
make them understand that difficult achievement of self-
knowledge, to know *what it is* to know; to give the first
attempted chart to guide them among the shallows and
rocks and whirlpools which beset the course and action
of thought and inquiry; to reveal to them the "idols"
which unconsciously haunt the minds of the strongest as
well as the weakest, and interpose their delusions when
we are least aware,—"the fallacies and false appearances
inseparable from our nature and our condition of life."
To induce men to believe not only that there was much
to know that was not yet dreamed of, but that the way
of knowing needed real and thorough improvement, that
the knowing mind bore along with it all kinds of snares
and disqualifications of which it is unconscious, and that
it needed training quite as much as materials to work
on, was the object of the *Advancement*.   It was but a
sketch; but it was a sketch so truly and forcibly drawn,
that it made an impression which has never been weak-
ened.   To us its use and almost its interest is passed.
But it is a book which we can never open without coming
on some noble interpretation of the realities of nature
or the mind; some unexpected discovery of that quick
and keen eye which arrests us by its truth; some felici-

tous and unthought-of illustration, yet so natural as
almost to be doomed to become a commonplace; some
bright touch of his incorrigible imaginativeness, ever
ready to force itself in amid the driest details of his
argument.

The *Advancement* was only one shape out of many
into which he cast his thoughts. Bacon was not easily
satisfied with his work; even when he published he did
so, not because he had brought his work to the desired
point, but lest anything should happen to him and it
should "perish." Easy and unstudied as his writing
seems, it was, as we have seen, the result of uninter-
mitted trouble and varied modes of working. He was
quite as much a talker as a writer, and beat out his
thoughts into shape in talking. In the essay on *Friendship* he describes the process with a vividness which
tells of his own experience :—

"But before you come to that [the faithful counsel that a man
receiveth from his friend], certain it is that whosoever hath his
mind fraught with many thoughts, his wits and understanding do
clarify and break up in the communicating and discoursing with
another. He tosseth his thoughts more easily; he marshalleth
them more orderly; he seeth how they look when they are turned
into words; finally, he waxeth wiser than himself, and that more
by an hour's discourse than by a day's meditation. It was well
said by Themistocles to the King of Persia, 'That speech was like
cloth of arras opened and put abroad, whereby the imagery doth
appear in figure; whereas in thought, they lie in packs.' Neither
is this second fruit of friendship, in opening the understanding,
restrained only to such friends as are able to give a man counsel.
(They are, indeed, best.) But even without that, a man learneth
of himself, and bringeth his own thoughts to light, and whetteth
his wits against a stone which itself cuts not. In a word, a man
were better relate himself to a *statua* or a picture, than to suffer his
thoughts to pass in smother."

Bacon, as has been said, was a great maker of notes
and note-books : he was careful not of the thought only
but of the very words in which it presented itself ;
everything was collected that might turn out useful in
his writing or speaking, down to alternative modes of
beginning or connecting or ending a sentence.   He
watched over his intellectual appliances and resources
much more strictly than over his money concerns.   He
never threw away and never forgot what could be turned
to account.   He was never afraid of repeating himself,
if he thought he had something apt to say.   He was
never tired of re-casting and re-writing, from a mere
fragment or preface to a finished paper.   He has
favourite images, favourite maxims, favourite texts,
which he cannot do without.   "*Da Fidei quæ sunt
Fidei*," comes in from his first book to his last.   The
illustrations which he gets from the myth of Scylla,
from Atalanta's ball, from Borgia's saying about the
French marking their lodgings with chalk, the saying
that God takes delight, like the "innocent play of
children," "to hide his works in order to have them
found out," and to have kings as "his playfellows in
that game," these, with many others, reappear, however
varied the context, from the first to the last of his
compositions.   An edition of Bacon with marginal
references and parallel passages would show a more
persistent recurrence of characteristic illustrations and
sentences than perhaps any other writer.

The *Advancement* was followed by attempts to give
serious effect to its lesson.   This was nearly all done in
Latin.   He did so, because in these works he spoke to a
larger and, as he thought, more interested audience ; the

use of Latin marked the gravity of his subject as one that
touched all mankind; and the majesty of Latin suited
his taste and his thoughts. Bacon spoke, indeed, impressively on the necessity of entering into the realm of knowledge in the spirit of a little child. He dwelt on the paramount importance of beginning from the very bottom of
the scale of fact, of understanding the commonplace things
at our feet, so full of wonder and mystery and instruction,
before venturing on theories. The sun is not polluted
by shining on a dunghill, and no facts were too ignoble
to be beneath the notice of the true student of nature.
But his own genius was for the grandeur and pomp of
general views. The practical details of experimental
science were, except in partial instances, yet a great way
off; and what there was, he either did not care about or
really understand, and had no aptitude for handling.
He knew enough to give reality to his argument; he
knew, and insisted on it, that the labour of observation
and experiment would have to be very heavy and quite
indispensable. But his own business was with great
principles and new truths; these were what had the
real attraction for him; it was the magnificent thoughts
and boundless hopes of the approaching kingdom of
man " which kindled his imagination and fired his ambition. " He writes philosophy," said Harvey, who had
come to his own great discovery through patient and
obscure experiments on frogs and monkeys, "he writes
philosophy like a Lord Chancellor." And for this part
of the work, the stateliness and dignity of the Latin
corresponded to the proud claims which he made for his
conception of the knowledge which was to be. English
seemed to him too homely to express the hopes of the

world, too unstable to be trusted with them.   Latin was
the language of command and law.   His Latin, without
enslaving itself to Ciceronian types, and with a free in-
fusion of barbarous but most convenient words from the
vast and ingenious terminology of the schoolmen, is
singularly forcible and expressive.   It is almost always
easy and clear; it can be vague and general, and it can
be very precise where precision is wanted.   It can, on
occasion, be magnificent, and its gravity is continually
enlivened by the play upon it, as upon a background, of
his picturesque and unexpected fancies.   The exposition
of his philosophical principles was attempted in two
forms.   He began in English.   He began, in the shape
of a personal account, a statement of a series of conclu-
sions·to which his thinking had brought him, which he
called the "Clue of the Labyrinth," *Filum Labyrinthi.*
But he laid this aside unfinished, and re-wrote and completed it in Latin, with the title *Cogitata et Visa.*   It
gains by being in Latin ; as Mr. Spedding says, "it must
certainly be reckoned among the most perfect of Bacon's
productions."   The personal form with each paragraph
begins and ends.   "*Franciscus Bacon sic cogitavit* . . .
itaque visum est ei," gives to it a special tone of serious
conviction, and brings the interest of the subject more
keenly to the reader.   It has the same kind of personal
interest, only more solemn and commanding, which there
is in Descartes's *Discours de la Méthode.*   In this form
Bacon meant at first to publish.   He sent it to his usual
critics, Sir Thomas Bodley, Toby Matthew, and Bishop
Andrewes.   And he meant to follow it up with a practical exemplification of his method.   But he changed
his plan.   He had more than once expressed his pre-

ference for the form of *aphorisms* over the argumentative
and didactic continuity of a set discourse. He had, indeed, already twice begun a series of aphorisms on the
true methods of interpreting nature, and directing the
mind in the true path of knowledge, and had begun
them with the same famous aphorism with which the
Novum Organum opens. He now reverted to the form
of the aphorism, and resolved to throw the materials of
the *Cogitata et Visa* into this shape. The result is the
Novum Organum. It contains, with large additions, the
substance of the treatise, but broken up and re-arranged
in the new form of separate impersonal generalised
observations. The points and assertions and issues
which, in a continuous discourse, careful readers mark
and careless ones miss, are one by one picked out and
brought separately to the light. It begins with brief,
oracular, unproved maxims and propositions, and goes
on gradually into larger developments and explanations.
The aphorisms are meant to strike, to awaken questions,
to disturb prejudices, to let in light into a nest of unsuspected intellectual confusions and self-misunderstand-
ings, to be the mottoes and watchwords of many a
laborious and difficult inquiry. They form a connected
and ordered chain, though the ties between each link are
not given. In this way Bacon put forth his proclamation of war on all that then called itself science ; his
announcement that the whole work of solid knowledge
must be begun afresh, and by a new, and, as he thought,
infallible method. On this work Bacon concentrated
all his care. It was twelve years in hand, and twelve
times underwent his revision. " In the first book especially," says Mr. Ellis, " every word seems to have been

carefully weighed; and it would be hard to omit or
change anything without injuring the meaning which
Bacon intended to convey." Severe as it is, it is instinct
with enthusiasm, sometimes with passion. The Latin
in which it is written answers to it; it has the concise-
ness, the breadth, the lordliness of a great piece of
philosophical legislation.

The world has agreed to date from Bacon the systematic reform of natural philosophy, the beginning of an
intelligent attempt, which has been crowned by such
signal success, to place the investigation of nature on a
solid foundation. On purely scientific grounds his title
to this great honour may require considerable qualifica-
tion. What one thing, it is asked, would not have been
discovered in the age of Galileo and Harvey, if Bacon
had never written? What one scientific discovery can
be traced to him, or to the observance of his peculiar
rules? It was something, indeed, to have conceived, as
clearly as he conceived it, the large and comprehensive
idea of what natural knowledge must be, and must rest
upon, even if he were not able to realise his idea, and
were mistaken in his practical methods of reform. But
great ideas and great principles need their adequate
interpreter, their *vates sacer*, if they are to influence the
history of mankind. This was what Bacon was to
science, to that great change in the thoughts and activity
of men in relation to the world of nature around them :
and this is his title to the great place assigned to him.
He not only understood and felt what science might be,
but he was able to make others—and it was no easy task
beforehand, while the wonders of discovery were yet in
the future—understand and feel it too. And he was

able to do this because he was one of the most wonderful
of thinkers and one of the greatest of writers. The
disclosure, the interpretation, the development of that
great intellectual revolution which was in the air, and
which was practically carried forward in obscurity, day
by day, by the fathers of modern astronomy and
chemistry and physiology, had fallen to the task of
a genius, second only to Shakespeare. He had the
power to tell the story of what they were doing and
were to do with a force of imaginative reason of which
they were utterly incapable. He was able to justify
their attempts and their hopes as they themselves could
not. He was able to interest the world in the great prospects opening on it, but of which none but a few students
had the key. The calculations of the astronomer, the
investigations of the physician, were more or less a subject of talk, as curious or possibly useful employments.
But that which bound them together in the unity of
science, which gave them their meaning beyond themselves, which raised them to a higher level and gave them
their real dignity among the pursuits of men, which
forced all thinking men to see what new and unsuspected
possibilities in the knowledge and in the condition of
mankind were opened before them, was not Bacon's
own attempts at science, not even his collections of
facts and his rules of method, but that great idea of the
reality and boundless worth of knowledge which Bacon's
penetrating and sure intuition had discerned, and
which had taken possession of his whole nature. The
impulse which he gave to the progress of science came
from his magnificent and varied exposition of this idea ;
from his series of grand and memorable generalisations

on the habits and faults of the human mind—on the difficult and yet so obvious and so natural precautions necessary to guide it in the true and hopeful track. It came from the attractiveness, the enthusiasm, and the persuasiveness of the pleading; from the clear and forcible statements, the sustained eloquence, the generous hopes, the deep and earnest purpose of the *Advancement* and the *De Augmentis;* from the nobleness, the originality, the picturesqueness, the impressive and irresistible truth of the great aphorisms of the *Novum Organum.*

THE END.

Printed by R. & R. CLARK, *Edinburgh.*

For EU product safety concerns, contact us at Calle de José Abascal, 56–1°,
28003 Madrid, Spain or eugpsr@cambridge.org.